Arab Unity and Disunity

Past and Present

Fuad Baali

University Press of America,® Inc.
Dallas · Lanham · Boulder · New York · Oxford

Library of Congress Control Number: 2004102953
ISBN 0-7618-2915-6 (paperback : alk. ppr.)

For my wife,
who gave up asking:
When will the Arabs unite?

"A group feeling [solidarity] that is stronger than all the other group feelings combined ... produces the ability to defend oneself, to offer opposition, to protect oneself, and to press one's claims."

Ibn Khaldun
(1332 -1406 A.D.)

CONTENTS

PREFACE

The idea of writing this book was suggested by the well-known Arab scholar Ali al-Wardi. In some of his published work, Wardi emphasized the important role of the nomadic *asabiyah* (solidarity, unity) in any federation, union, or unity of the Arab states. Chapters One and Two concern Arab unity and disunity before, during, and after Mohammed's time. They show the conflict between, as well as the compatibilty of, the ideals of the old nomadic life and the spirit of Islam. The historical perspective helps us understand the ups and downs of Arab solidarity. Without this approach, it would be difficult to know the roots of divisiveness, rivalries, and disputes that continue among the Arabs until present day. Chapter Three deals mainly with the factors contributing to recent Arab unity and disunity. Chapter Four analyzes the reasons for the inability of the Arabs to replace their local and narrow *asabiyahs* with the wider, more comprehensive, Arab unity.

As in the other published work of this writer, objectivity has been maintained throughout this book.

F. G. Baali
Bowling Green, Kentucky
January 2004

Chapter 1

ISLAM AND THE ARABS:
BACKGROUND OF THE UPS AND DOWNS OF UNITY*

Some modern students of Islam believe that the teaching of Islam runs contrary to the cultural pattern of the Arabian nomads,[1] and that it was Mohammed who first maintained this attitude "with persistent energy."[2] We believe that this explanation is not entirely true. We find no fundamental difference between the spirit of Islam and that of Arab nomadism. It may be quite safe to generalize that all the religions which arise in secular societies tend to derive their fundamental principles from the ideals of the sacred society. Hence the disintegration of social life under the impact of the secularization process seems to be one of the main reasons for the rise of the great prophets. The strong solidarity of the sacred society and the feeling of brotherhood among its members are emphasized by the great religions of the world, including Islam. Islam has emphasized that its followers should act toward each other like brothers.[3] In one of his sayings Mohammed declared that "mankind is the family of Allah, and so, the most beloved man in the sight of Allah is that who is most helpful to His family."[4] The Hebrew prophets, whom Mohammed admired, were in fact vehement critics of the moral disintegration and social secularization of ancient civilization. They were, in other words, preaching the ideals of the old nomadic life after it had been replaced by a sedentary one in Palestine. In the words of H. G. Wells, "They kept up the nomadic traditions as against the 'new ways' of settlements."[5]

The Arab nomadic society was, and still is, highly integrated within the tribal unit. Brotherhood, cooperation, and loyalty hold among the members of the tribe, rich or poor, powerful or powerless. The Arab is, as Hitti points out, "a born democrat,"[6] but when he meets men from other tribes he becomes ethnocentric.[7] He looks upon his tribe as the best and the most honorable one in the world. Herein lies the main source of conflict between Islam and Arab nomadism. In the eyes of the nomads, man must be loyal to his tribesmen, but not to others. According to the Mohammedan point of view, however, all the tribes within the boundaries of the Islamic community are equal. With one stroke Mohammed shifts the center of loyalty from the tribe to the community of religion: "All of you are the children of Adam, and Adam was created from the dust of the earth. The best among you is, then, the most pious of you."[8]

We believe that the five pillars of Islam[9] are intended to combat the nomadic tribal spirit *(asabiyah)*.[10] Non-Muslim observers are often astonished at the rigidity of these Islamic pillars, which consume so much of the Muslim's time. Some modern thinkers regard them as obstacles which handicap the Muslims in their secular activities. These complicated and difficult pillars of Islam, however, were indeed meaningful in the early days of Islam. They were meant to weaken the *tribal* pride of the Arabs.   Ali, the fourth caliph, was perhaps the first man to discover the social meaningfulness of the pillars along these lines. In this opinion, to prostrate oneself in prayer and put one's face on the dust of the earth, to fast from sunrise to sunset everyday for a whole month, and the like, are all intended to train man to be humble toward his fellow men and submissive toward God.[11]

According to Muir, Islam was not meant to be a universal religion, for Mohammed's world was Arabia, and for Arabia Islam was sent. "From the first to the last the call was made primarily to the Arabs and to them alone."[12] Arnold, however, argues that Islam was never designed for the Arabs alone. "As there was but one God, so there was to be but one religion in which all men were to be invited."[13] Khadduri also points out that *The Koran* and the history of Mohammed support Arnold's view that Islam was meant to be a universal religion.[14] We believe that both Muir's and Arnold's opinions are valid. Each represents a single phase of the multiphased reality, but not the whole of it. It is true that Islam is a universal religion sent to the various peoples of the world;[15] but it is also true that most of the ideals, values, pillars, and beliefs of Islam are built on an Arabic foundation and designed to satisfy certain Arabic needs.

One cannot deny the fact that Mohammed was himself an Arab, and his mission was greatly colored by the values and thought-style of nomadic culture. Although the quality Mohammed disliked most was extreme loyalty to the tribe, the sacred society of the nomadic tribe provided him with most of his moral values. In fact, Mohammed is known to have said, "Men are like minerals— those who were good before Islam are equally good in Islam."[16] He also said, "Look to those moral practices you had before the coming of Islam and apply them to Islam; give security to your guest, be generous toward the orphan, and treat your neighbor with kindness."[17] A similar sentiment can be found in *The Koran*.[18] We are told that Hatim's[19] daughter was led as a captive before the Prophet and addressed him thus: "My father was wont to free the captive, and protect those near and dear to him, and entertain the guest, and satisfy the hungry, and console the afflicted, and give food and greetings to all; and never did he turn away any who sought a boon." The Prophet answered her: "O maiden, the true believer is such as thou has described. . . ." He then turned to his followers and said: "Let her go free for her sire loved noble manners, and God loves them likewise."[20]

In dealing with the fundamentals of their religion, Muslim theologians have distinguished among *believing, worshipping,* and *right-doing.*[21] To them Islam primarily consists of these three elements. In the light of the preceding discussion, we believe that the first two elements were most probably instituted by Mohammed for the purpose of weakening the Arab tribal spirit, whereas the third element, right-doing, was instituted in order to retain and strengthen their moral values. Mohammed is popularly known to have said that he was sent by Allah for the purpose of "completing" the good morals.[22]

Nicholson points out that although the Arabs "became Moslems *en masse,* the majority of them neither believed in Islam nor knew what it meant."[23] Generally speaking, Nicholson's conclusion can be called right only in relation to the tribal spirit. The Arabs seemed to be unable to replace the age-old narrow spirit of the tribe with the wider spirit of the Islamic community. In spite of the Prophet's persistent condemnation of the tribal spirit, the Arabs continued to be, consciously or unconsciously, influenced by it. This may be attributed to the fact that some cultural traditions and mores may not be easily overcome by new systems of belief and worship. When the Arab tribal spirit *(asabiyah)* coincided with certain aspects of religion, however, the Arabs became extremely religious. They actually showed amazing zeal, sincerity, and devotion to Islam when immediately after the Prophet's death their *asabiyah* was directed against the "unbelievers" outside Arabia. Therefore, the assertions by some modern historians that the Arabs were then merely fighting with a utilitarian motive and that their ends were secular rather than sacred[24] cannot be entirely accepted. Some were seeking mere booty and plunder, but the majority were sacrificing their own lives in what they firmly believed to be a holy war. It is true that what chiefly inspired the Arabs in their religious vehemence was their success in fighting against the "unbelievers,"[25] but this should not be taken as a flat indication of utilitarianism or materialism. The nomads, or for that matter any sacred society, do not separate might from right. As long as men are on the side of God, He must be on their side, too.

We believe, then, that the oft-mentioned antagonism between Islam and the Arab values developed later, when Islam began to be adopted by civilized peoples of the conquered territories. It is reasonable to suggest that the conquered peoples adopted Islam after they changed it to fit their own social and psychic needs.

1.   *The Asabiyah (unity) in Islam*
In order to extend the boundary of Islam, Mohammed tried to suppress the narrow tribal spirit of the nomads and install in its place the religious spirit. He vehemently attacked the nomadic pride in genealogy and preached that zeal for faith was the only criterion of honor. It was difficult, however, for the nomads to abandon so quickly the tribal spirit to which they had been

accustomed since the beginning of their known history. As Levy puts it, "it is obvious that so intangible an element in social organization as a feeling of pride in ancestry was not be destroyed by edict at one stroke."[26] Soon after the Prophet died, many tribes renounced the newly organized state of Islam and followed a number of local "false" prophets.[27] Some of the Arabs flatly declared that a "false prophet from our own tribe is better than a true one from the tribe of Quraysh."[28] The tribal spirit was one of the main factors underlying the nomadic revolt against the Islamic rule.

The reins of the Islamic government after the Prophet's death were placed in the hands of Umar Ibn al-Khattab, who seemed to have a great capacity for penetrating into the deep nature of the Arabs.[29] After suppressing the uprising of the defectors, he seems to have realized that unless the Arabs' attention could be diverted by some positive activities and to a new sort of loyalty, their old tribal spirit would continue to stir trouble. Thus, the historic wars of conquest, which were waged shortly after the Prophet's death, can be regarded as a strategy to replace the tribal raids and the internal wars of the desert by an organized campaign against the outsiders. History tells us that Umar converted all of Arabia into a military camp. He expelled the non-Arabs from the Arabian Peninsula as if he intended to free it from the danger of a fifth column. In his words the Arabian nomads "furnished Islam with its raw material."[30] It appeared as if he had attempted to make the Arabs identical with the Muslims and Arabism synonymous with Islam.[31] In fact, there are several sayings attributed to Umar, which indicate his personal inclination toward the Arabs and his appreciation for their cultural values. He is known even to have urged the Arabs to preserve their traditional pride in genealogy.[32] He did not intend, however, to strengthen Arabism at the expense of the religious spirit. In fact, for military purposes Umar mobilized the Arabian nomads along tribal lines[33] so as to make the nomadic spirit *(asabiyah)* identical with the Islamic spirit. The *asabiyah* was not entirely eliminated; it was, rather, put into a new and temporary form. When the conquests practically ceased after the death of Umar and during the reign of the third caliph Uthman, the *asabiyah* began to appear again and play its role in the political affairs of Islam.

Generally, Muslim historians tend to consider the death of Umar (who was murdered by a Persian while leading the prayers in the great Mosque of Medina in A.D. 644) one of the greatest calamities in the history of Islam. In the words of one historian, "the good fortune of Islam was shrouded in the grave-clothes of Umar."[34] Historians agree that most of the turmoil and social unrest which took place during the reign of Uthman would not have happened had Umar lived longer. This is, to some extent, true. Umar was, as Nicholson points out, "a born ruler and every inch a man," whereas his successor, Uthman, was "an easy tool in the hands of his ambitious kinsfolk."[35] It seems, however, that historians overestimate the personal factor in history and underestimate the social factor, which we believe is a more important force. We believe also that the halting of conquests was much more effective in causing social unrest than the personal weakness of the caliph. The tribal *asabiyah,* which was directed at the time of Umar against the "unbelievers," simply turned back to its old pattern once the holy wars slowed down at the time of Uthman.

Uthman practiced nepotism. His relatives, who formed the leading family of the tribe of Quraysh, climbed into most of the lucrative and important offices of the newly established empire and lived on the fat of the land.[36] This naturally drew the attention, and probably the envy, of the other tribes. The trouble might have been less had the relatives of Uthman been considered true Muslims. "Their ungodly behavior," says Nicholson, gave point to the question whether these converts of the eleventh hour were not still heathens at heart."[37] The other tribes seemed to have found the situation unbearable. There was, of course, fertile soil for the old tribal spirit to flourish again. History shows that the first instance of trouble against Uthman's regime arose in Iraq as a result of a heated conversation between certain tribesmen and the governor of Iraq, who was a Qurayshite and a close relative of Uthman. During the conversation, the governor declared that Iraq was an "orchard" of the tribe of Quraysh and that the Qurayshites had a right to reap its produce any time they wanted. The tribesmen vehemently protested this, saying that what had been conquered by their own swords could not easily be permitted to be exploited by the tribe of Quraysh alone.[38] This event can be considered the beginning of the turmoil against Uthman. His rivals made full use of this hostility to their own advantage. In some of their letters to the indignant tribesmen they said that, "if you want a holy war, come here, for the religion of Mohammed has been spoiled by your caliph."[39] Many tribesmen responded favorably to these letters and went to Medina, where Uthman lived, seeking a cause for a holy war. Uthman summoned the governors and the politicians from the various parts of the empire to discuss with them the causes of, and a remedy for, the upheaval. One of the conferees flatly advised the caliph to start new campaigns against foreign people in order to direct the warlike energy of the tribes outward.[40] An Arab poet, who lived at the time in which these events took place, had this to say: "Our business is to make raids on the enemy, on our neighbor and on our brother, in case we find none to raid but a brother!"[41]

When Uthman was finally besieged in his house by the indignant Arabs, one of his cousins, Marwan, came out of the house and addressed the excited besiegers in a way that seemed to reduce the rebellion against his cousin to a mere raid against his tribe. That Marwan's interpretation of the raid was correct became clearer after the murder of Uthman at the hands of his besiegers. The relatives of Uthman considered his murder a family concern rather than a political one. They abstained from giving their oath of allegiance to Ali, who succeeded Uthman in the caliphate, on the grounds that he did not avenge the murdered caliph.[42] Thus the historic conflict between Ali and Mu'awiyah began.[43]

The clash between Ali and Mu'awiyah was regarded by some orthodox Muslims as an example of the age-old conflict between right and might, the ideal and the real, politics and religion. Many historians believe that one of the main reasons for the failure of Ali in his war against Mu'awiyah was his failure to pay attention to the tribal spirit *(asabiyah)*. He treated all people equally, according to the original spirit of Islam. He did not prefer the Arabs to the non-Arabs, and he did not cajole the leaders and the chiefs of the tribes.[44] Mu'awiyah, on the other hand, based his whole policy on the expediency of the tribal spirit. He divided the public revenue neither equally as Ali did nor according to religious merit as Umar maintained but according to what Ibn Khaldun calls the principles of *asabiyah*. Therefore, strong tribes had a bigger share in the budget of Mu'awiyah.[45] It is significant to note that the tribe of Quraysh disliked Ali, and he himself disliked it,[46] in spite of the fact that he belonged to one of its leading families. He can be said to have led, in a sense, the religious opposition against the tribal spirit of Quraysh.

In this conflict between Ali and Mu'awiyah, we can observe a peculiar phenomenon to which historians have not paid much attention. Strothmann points out that the early Shiites, that is, the partisans of Ali, were mostly from the southern part of Arabia.[47] Zaydan also shows that the historic battle which raged between Ali and Mu'awiayh in Siffin was regarded at the time as a war between the southern Arabs (or the Yemenites, as they were usually called) and Quraysh.[48] Why should the Yemenites have been so peculiarly attached to the cause of Ali? An examination of their social background provides a simple answer. Unlike the northern part of Arabia, southern Arabia or Yemen had a long history of sedentary life and thus did not pay attention to tribal spirit. This may explain how the Yemenites could endure the rule of Ali which neglected the tribal spirit. We believe, however, that while the northerners had a "group religion," the Yemenites persisted in their partisanship for Ali long after his death. Mu'awiyah tried to suppress this tendency, using persecution and bribery to draw them to his side. In contrast to the more Arabian nomads to the north, the Yemenites seemed to have believed that might was not a necessary phase of right; hence their adherence to the cause of Ali in spite of his defeat in war and failure in politics.

It is interesting to note that certain northern tribes also sided with Ali; but as soon as they spotted the first signs of his failure they seceded from his side and formed the Kharijites (the Seceders) sect. The Kharijites began to fight both Ali and Mu'awiyah. They fought Ali because he had failed in war,[49] and fought Mu'awiyah probably because he was biased in favor of the tribe of Quraysh. Thus they showed the deep-rooted characteristics of their nomadic nature. Historians are often amazed at the apparently trivial reason which caused them to secede from Ali's side after being deeply devoted, in the beginning, to his cause. The Kharijites believed that Ali was good and just as far as he was victorious and that his defeat was an indication that Allah had quit his side.[50] Ali condemned this identification of might with right. In his opinion, if might and right always go together there will be no way of distinguishing the sincere believer from the pretender, for the reward of Allah is given according to how much the believer has suffered for the sake of his faith. Ali provides several examples from the history of religion to prove his point, including the fact that the true prophets attracted only a few disciples in the beginning, but afterwards they were able to found their great religions as a result of their efforts, patience, and suffering.[51] It is, of course, difficult for the Arabian nomads to understand this type of thinking since they cannot imagine right without might behind it. The nomad firmly believes that the only righteous group in the world is his tribe. His passionate attachment to his tribe is usually associated with an indubitable belief that the deity, whatever it may be, is always standing by its side. He cannot understand how a true religion goes against his tribe. When the nomads rally to the help of their fellow tribesmen against strangers, they are confident that their tribe is always right. It seems that the severe struggle for existence in the desert life has taught him that the mere survival of his tribe indicates its rightfulness.

The Kharijites provide us with a good example of this nomadic tendency. They are well known for their extreme piety and devotion to Islam,[52] yet they did not hesitate to kill the women and children of their enemies and to plunder their property wherever they found them. In their opinion "Muslims who refused to execrate Uthman and Ali were the worst of infidels; it was the duty of every true believer to take part in the Holy War against such, and to kill them, together with their wives and children."[53] In this respect, then, the Kharijites were not greatly different from the nomads of the pre-Islamic days. The only difference between these two groups lies in the fact that the former had many gods (each tribe had its own god that stood on its side against the others), whereas the latter believed in only one God, who was supposed to support them against the whole world on account of their great worship and devotion.[54]

In spite of their extreme piety and devotion to Allah, the Kharijites could not understand the egalitarian principle of Islam. They revolted against the tribal spirit of Quraysh and retained, at the same time, their own. According to Amin, they had a great pride in their pedigree, and an intense contempt for non-Arab Muslims.[55]

After the establishment of the Umayyad dynasty, the Kharijites gradually began to withdraw from Iraq, where their movement first started, to the desert, that is, to their original abode, where it was easier to preserve their nomadic-religious values. The rising tide of social secularization and civilization in Islam appeared to have worked against them. Remnants of the Kharijites can be found today in certain isolated areas of the Arabian and African deserts.

At any rate, the Umayyads found it necessary to resume the war against the outside world. A great series of foreign conquests, second to that of Umar, was achieved during their reign. The Arab soldiers reached the frontiers of China to the east and penetrated France to the west. As a result of this contact with various peoples, two kinds of spirit began to develop: first, the spirit which distinguished the northern Arabs from the southern Arabs; second, the spirit which combined all the Arabs against the non-Arabs.

The Umayyads persistently sided with the Arabs against the non-Arabs. Theirs was in reality a rule of Arabs for Arabs.[56] The Arabs began to form an aristocratic class and to look down upon their non-Arab subject.[57] This was one of the main reasons for the undermining of the Umayyad regime in particular and Arab rule in general; another factor was the conflict between the northern and the southern Arabs.

2.   *The Nature of Islam*

As a result of the fall of the Umayyad dynasty, Islam began to be molded anew mainly by the non-Arab converts; Islam began to erase the values of nomadism.

During the Abbasid caliphate, the Mohammedan Traditions began to be collected and organized in their final forms. The Traditionists developed then *ilm al-hadith* (the science of Traditions). The purpose of this discipline was to sift the true Traditions from among the thousands which were attributed to Mohammed and his companions. The traditionists, however, did not care to examine the text of the Tradition to see whether or not it was reasonable and logical. In their opinion, the Prophet's sayings were inspired by God, and so man was not permitted to examine them in the light of his limited mind. Their main job, therefore, was to examine the integrity of those who carried the Traditions.[58]

Generally the Traditionists classify the bearers of Traditions according to their truthfulness and honesty on the one hand and according to their partisanship toward certain heretical sects or unpopular parties on the other. By doing that, they are in reality examining the reasonableness of the Traditions in the light of their own logical system or presuppositions. Thus Traditions are in reality sifted in a manner which eliminates all but those that fit into Traditionist rules of logical reasoning. Looking for prejudice in their opponents, they are unable to notice it in themselves.

We can understand, then, how the nature of Islam was finally colored by values of civilization. We can find in Islam, even at that time, some aspects which run contrary to the basic tendencies of nomadism. Let us examine two important ones:

1. Whereas the nomad had a profound contempt for intellectual learning,[59] there was a deep-rooted inclination in Islam toward scientific knowledge of all sorts. According to the Traditionists, Mohammed urged his

followers to seek scientific knowledge. There are many traditions indicating the high position of science (in the opinion of the Prophet).[60] From Mohammed's perspective, however, the meaning of the word "science" *(ilm)* is somewhat different from that which the Traditionists have used under the influence of civilization. We believe that Mohammed considered *ilm* the opposite of *jahl* (ignorance; from which the term *Jahiliyah* was derived). It is quite possible, therefore, that *ilm* in the Prophet's terminology means "the understanding of the moral or religious rules of conduct."[61]

2. The nomadic people despised professions and abased men who depended for their livelihood on jobs and occupations because, in their opinion, these men were weak and subjected by others. The nomads, instead, would fight and raid. As Ibn Khaldun puts it, they prefer to earn their living by the points of their spears.[62] The Muslim Traditionists believe that Mohammed enthusiastically encouraged agriculture and craftsmanship. There is, however, one tradition which seems to condemn agriculture and regard it as a cause of humiliation.[63] The Traditionists were puzzled as to its real meaning.[64] They seemed to be unable to realize that Mohammed was not entirely free from the nomadic values; they seemed to impose their own values on the Prophet.

Regardless of their views on occupations and related matters, the Arabs, whether nomadic or sedentary, shared, and still value highly, the sense of personal dignity, which is so strong that they are "naturally in revolt against every form of authority."[65] This may explain why the *Arabs before Mohammed were unable to unite* themselves and form a state. As we have seen before, through the idea of one impersonal God, *Mohammed was able to unite them.* Furthermore, he was in the habit of referring to his orders as those of God Himself. To quote H. G. Wells, "Muhammed was no imposter, at any rate, though at times his vanity made him behave as though Allah was at his beck and call, and as if his thoughts were necessarily God's thoughts."[66] We believe that Mohammed's frequent reference to Allah can be more readily interpreted as a social technique to make the Arabs react favorably toward the new authority of Islam. It can be regarded, in other words, as a technique for the depersonalization of the Mohammedan authority.[67] Because of the Arab's sensitivity to all sorts of authority, Mohammed had to avoid the appearance of giving personal orders. When the newly converted chief of an Arab tribe said to the Prophet, "You are our prince," the Prophet answered quickly, "The prince is Allah, not I."[68] In this way he was able to establish the virtually unquestioned authority of Islam over Arabia. At any rate, Mohammed appeared to have been fully aware of the great danger inherent in this tendency of the Arabs to revolt against authority. In fact, he tried to teach his followers that it was their duty to obey their ruler whoever he might be.[69] Mohammed condemned also all sorts of arrogance and any undue sense of personal dignity. *The Koran* describes the true Muslims as "those who walk on earth humbly and, when offended by insolent people, reply peaceably."[70]

A dilemma arose, however, when the Arabs were enlisted into the conquering armies of Islam. It was difficult for the Arabs to be peaceful and humble and retain at the same time their propensity for fighting. Some historians seem unaware of this sociologically important dilemma. Immediately after the Prophet's death, some of his companions who belonged to the early group of converts retired from political life and began practicing religious activities privately, believing that Islam should no longer be concerned with military or political affairs.[71] This historical event is important; it indicates the inner conflict which appeared within the souls of pious Muslims (owing to the rise of the above-mentioned dilemma). Finally, as we have already seen, Umar took the lead and directed Islam toward the path of war and conquest. As a matter of fact, Umar adopted several positive measures which clearly indicated his policy of directing Islam toward the politico-militant spirit rather than toward peaceful devotion. Let us examine them one by one.

1. A change in the traditional call for prayer. The call contained, before Umar's time, a sentence intended to remind the Muslims that the prayer was the best of all religious activities. Umar ordered the omission of this sentence from the call. He might have noticed in it a sort of encouragement for a peaceful life. Sharaf al-Din believes that Umar was urging Muslims to concentrate their attention and devotion upon the war activity; and so, he might have seen in the sentence a cause of deviation from this direction.[72]

2. Prohibition of the Arabs from agricultural activities. Umar even prevented them from living in towns or mixing with town populations. Alayili believes that this action was contrary to the orders of the Prophet, but Umar had to do it in order to make the Arabs retain their old warlike spirit and fighting vehemence.[73]

3. The arrangement of the Islamic armies along tribal lines.[74] Umar also warned them against adoption of the customs of the outsiders.[75]

4. The appointment of those Ibn Khaldun calls the holders of the *asabiyah* to government and military offices.[76] Many offices were filled during his reign with certain members of the Umayyad family, while the Hashimid family (of Mohammed and Ali) was avoided in these appointments. Some famous Muslim historians, for example, Al-Maqrizi, were appalled by such discrimination.[77] The discrimination may not lie in the personal hatred of Umar for Ali, but in the general policy of Umar to use the tribal and the warlike spirit of the Arabs to enhance the Islamic victories. The Umayyads, unlike Ali and his followers, were strongly inclined toward the Arabian nomads' values. As a result, Islam became a religion of conquests and empire-building rather than one of submissive devotion and humble piety. The holy war was, as Khadduri points out, a "required duty" imposed on the whole Islamic community to make the word of Allah supreme in the world.[78] This has placed the Traditionists face to face with a dilemma of their own. As civilized men, they are oriented toward a

religion of humbleness and devotion, but, as orthodox Muslims, they are required to believe in the holy war against "unbelievers," wherever they are.[79] How have they been able to escape these two sharp horns of the dilemma? It seems that the Traditionists have found the solution in what can be called "the depersonalization of human traits." In their opinion, man can attain through the exertion of his willpower any trait he likes. With the help of Allah, human personality can be molded to fit every form, with no restriction whatsoever. To them, Mohammed and his companions were exactly as *The Koran* has described them—severe against the "unbelievers," compassionate among themselves. It should be stated here that the later generations failed to follow this high example of the companions partly because of their weak will and weak religious beliefs and partly because the dilemma was no longer significant. Islam then had yielded to the soft proclivities of civilization and, accordingly, lost its tendency to fight. The duty of holy war had lost its actual value; it became a mere word in the religious terminology.

Islam as a militant religion remains only in the desert. Recently, religious movements have developed in the Arabian and African deserts, attempting to revive Islam along Umar's pattern.[80] They have succeeded only within the desert boundaries. The reason behind the inability of the nomads to invade modern civilization lies perhaps in the fact that civilization is today no longer an abode of submissive peoples, as Ibn Khaldun claims.

3.   *Ibn Khaldun on Nomadism and Civilization*
Ibn Khaldun classifies human society, from the standpoint of social control, into two types: *badawa and hadarah* (primitive and civilized or nomadism and urbanism). In the *badawa*, where blood relationship prevails, people are controlled by their own spontaneous motivation. Among the nomads, the tribal spirit or *asabiyah*[81] enhances group values. In the *hadarah*, on the other hand, force, for example, that of police, is necessary as a form of social control.

Through this classification, Ibn Khaldun places the *asabiyah* of the nomads in general, and of the Arabs in particular, in a favorable position. No writer before Ibn Khaldun was able to defend it or to show its advantage.

Ibn Khaldun points out that man's qualities are the result of his social condition.[82] In discussing the qualities distinguishing the civilized man from the nomad, for example, the scientific inclination, craftsmanship, and humility as against the nomadic illiteracy, predatory spirit, and pride, Ibn Khaldun comes to the conclusion that civilized people are by no means better than nomads. The strong *asabiyah* seems to compensate, in his opinion, for all the virtues of civilization.

There is indeed a great similarity between Ibn Khaldun's description of the nomadic *asabiyah* and Durkheim's description of mechanical social solidarity. While Durkheim believes that the rate of suicide rises as a result of the weakening of mechanical solidarity, Ibn Khaldun believes that the weakening of the *asabiyah* among civilized people indicates the approaching suicide of the society as a whole.

The spirit which makes the members of a group strongly attached to each other against strangers makes them, at the same time, strongly attached to the values of the group. Strong tribal spirit and strong morals seems to go hand in hand in Ibn Khaldun's theory. To him, the nomads have strong morals and thus are closer to the spirit of religion than are civilized people. Vice and moral laxity, which prevail in civilization, are rare in nomadism. He attributes the prevalence of vice and wickedness in civilization to the use of force as a form of social control. As a matter of fact, Ibn Khaldun's inclination in favor of nomadism can be more or less clearly observed throughout his work:

1. He seems to prefer nomadism on the basis of his values (concerning human nature). To him, man is good and bad at the same time.[83] Man's badness is due to his being an animal in his original[84] nature, and his goodness, on the other hand, comes from his association with other men.[85] From this one can conclude that Ibn Khaldun believes that the stronger the attachment of man to his group the better he becomes, for his social nature will be strengthened at the expense of his animal nature. Here, Ibn Khaldun emphasizes the process of socialization, specifically the importance of association with others. In this he stands in opposition to the Traditionists, who have depersonalized human traits.

2. Another reason why Ibn Khaldun prefers nomadism lies in the fact that nomads are more capable than others of fighting and conquering other peoples. Man is naturally inclined to master others.[86] A submissive man is imperfect, and yielding to humiliation of any kind indicates defectiveness in the essence of manhood. In this respect the nomad is, in comparison to the civilized person, superior.[87]

3. Ibn Khaldun also notes that the use of forces as a means of social control makes man liable to be untruthful and a cheater.[88] In order to evade the oppression of government, the civilized man tends to hide his real nature.[89] The nomadic man, on the other hand, does not like to conceal himself; he is afraid of no one. A coward cannot survive in the desert.

4. Ibn Khaldun also notes that civilization is usually associated with tendencies toward luxury. Luxury leads to cheating, gambling, stealing, adultery, false swearing, usury, and so forth. When man finds himself in urgent need of money in order to satisfy the various wants of his luxurious life, he may be obliged to use illegitimate means to get it. With the passage of time, bad morals will prevail in civilization.[90]

5. The existence of commerce and craftsmanship in civilization necessarily requires cunning and deception. This characteristic is remote from that of manliness.[91]

6.   The nomads can quite readily adapt themselves to religious discipline and asceticism. They usually wear simple clothes, live in simple houses, and eat simple food. This means, of course, that there is less entanglement in worldly affairs.[92]

Nevertheless, Ibn Khaldun does not admire the nomadic culture without reservation. He is, in fact, quite aware of the existence of certain "bad" traits among the nomads. He has distinguished himself from other students of the nomadic culture, however, by viewing these bad traits as inherent by-products of good traits.[93] In other words he has not accepted the depersonalization of human traits which the orthodox writers have maintained. Ibn Khaldun does not treat social phenomena according to the law of the excluded middle, as orthodox writers usually do. In other words, he does not view them as dichotomies in which absolute good is set against absolute evil;[94] rather, he arranges social phenomena along a continuum. From this perspective he views the whole pattern of the nomadic culture as well as the type of personality which normally prevails in it.

Ibn Khaldun seems to conclude that since the nomadic man is braver, stronger, and more capable of fighting than the civilized man, he must also be more arrogant and less obedient to the rules of an orderly life. According to Ibn Khaldun's definition of the perfect man, the nomad is the most perfect man on earth; but he is also the greatest troublemaker. The nomad can easily establish a state with his sword, but he reluctantly submits to its rules.[95]

When Ibn Khaldun discusses the nature of the Arab Bedouins of his time he emphatically shows that they are the most difficult people to rule. They tend to envy, rival, dispute, and fight one another as soon as they are in proximity. When they see any sign of weakness in their leader, they quickly move to compete with him for the leadership.[96] Their only bond is their strong *asabiyah* which Ibn Khaldun considers a natural tendency in man. Man generally tends to be kind and helpful to his relatives; and he will naturally feel insulted if a member of his family or clan is insulted by an outsider.[97]

It is advantageous for a desert tribe to be large; the larger the tribe, the greater opportunity it has to survive at the expense of other tribes. A nomadic tribe likes to increase its population by every possible means, but there is a built-in limit on this tendency. As soon as a tribe reaches a certain size, the nomadic attitudes of envy and arrogance tend to break it up into smaller units. This leads Ibn Khaldun to say also that *the Arabs are unable to establish a state or successfully manage it without a religion*. Their pride and roughness normally make it difficult for them to be unified into a large state; but when the various tribe submit, under the influence of religion, to one authority, they can achieve miracles.[98] Their roughness then will be directed against the outsiders. Ibn Khaldun is inclined toward a "group religion" rather than a "class religion," toward a "church" type rather than a "sect" type of religion. He believes that the social function of religion is to unify the group rather than weaken it. He seems to believe that the purpose of true religion is not to change or reform the mores of the people. Mores form an inevitable aspect of the social situation in which the people happen to exist. True religion, therefore, merely tries to eliminate fratricidal hostility in order to make people one solid body against their enemies. The Arab nomads are, by nature, well prepared to adapt themselves to the moral discipline of religion; they are free from the moral disorganization of civilization. Religion also makes them give up their nomadic roughness.[99]

It is interesting to find Ibn Khaldun, in various parts of his work, emphasizing the idea that *religion without asabiyah is ineffective.*[100] He seems to believe that a religion without followers who are capable of fighting and conquering is useless or perhaps false. To him a true religion has to be a victorious one. It may be safe to conclude here that, in his opinion, nomadism and religion are highly compatible; each is useless without the other. The nomads are scattered, rough beings until religion comes and makes them victorious. In the same way, religion is an impotent system of ideas until the nomads adopt it and make it a tangible system of social order. In brief, religion and nomadism, or right and might, cannot be separated, according to his theory. They are necessary to each other.

Consequently, Ibn Khaldun has to face the multitude of Mohammedan Traditions, which positively condemn the nomadic traits. It should be pointed out that he usually overlooks the Traditions that contradict his theory and unduly emphasizes those which can be used in its support.[101] At any rate, he seems to be unable to proceed along these vulnerable lines to the extreme. He cannot particularly refute the Traditions unanimously considered valid by the orthodox Muslims, for this would invalidate the principle of *ijma* (unanimity) of which he himself is a vehement advocate. He must, therefore, resort to some other means. Let us see how Ibn Khaldun examines these Traditions.

1. It is a well established Tradition in Islam that Mohammed urged his followers to quit the desert and adopt city life.[102] Ibn Khaldun points out that this Tradition does not represent a permanent order which should be executed at all times and places. The reason why the Prophet after *hijrah* (migration to Medina) urged his followers to join him in Medina was to mobilize them against the unbelievers. It is therefore a temporary order; it has no meaning after the victory.[103]

2. The Prophet is known to have encouraged and praised agriculture; there are several Traditions to this effect. Ibn Khaldun seems to regard them as meaningless or insignificant. He mentions only one Tradition condemning agriculture. The Traditionists have agreed that there must be something wrong with this Tradition, and so they have not accepted it at its face value. In spite of this, Ibn Khaldun takes it seriously in order to support his own argument that agriculture is an occupation adopted only by humble and weak people, and thus

the strong nomads do not wish to be cultivators and payers of taxes.[104]

3.   The nomadic *asabiyah* is to a great extent condemned by the Prophet, as we have already seen. Ibn Khaldun believes that this condemnation is not directed against the *asabiyah* as such[105] but against the *asabiyah* of the pre-Islamic days which was generally used in intertribal wars and raids. The *asabiyah,* like any other human trait, can be good or bad, depending on the purpose for which it is used. It can be good if it is used for a good purpose, for example, to support religion or to maintain justice, or it can be bad if it is used for the purpose of maintaining self-interest or supporting an unjust cause.[106]

4.   The Prophet condemned also the nomad's pride in lineage; he considered all men equal regardless of their lineage or background. *The Koran* says, "O ye folk, verily we have created you of male and female... . Verily the most honorable of you in the sight of Allah is the most pious of you."[107] Moreover, the Prophet is known to have said, "There are no genealogies in Islam."[108]   In Ibn Khaldun's opinion, pride in genealogy is a natural tendency in man. It is also the basis of tribal spirit; if pride in genealogy is weak, tribal spirit is weak, too. He attributes the fall of the Arabs to their mixture with non-Arabs, a phenomenon that led them to neglect their celebrated genealogy. To support this explanation, he cites a saying from Umar urging the Arabs to keep their genealogy.[109]   As we have already noted, Umar views genealogy from the same perspective as does Ibn Khaldun.   Both are inclined to see the Arabs as conquerors over other nations.

Along these lines Ibn Khaldun has defended the Arabs. Because Islam had been already institutionalized according to the values of civilization, and because the Arabs had been unable to express themselves again through widespread conquest, the voice of Ibn Khaldun was therefore like a cry in the wilderness.

NOTES

* In association with Ali al-Wardi.

1. See for example, R. A. Nicholson, *A Literary History of the Arabs* (Cambridge: University Press, 1930), pp. 177-78; I. Goldziher, *Al-Madhahib al-Islamiyah fi Tafsir al-Koran* (Cairo: Ulum Press, 1944); A. Amin, *Fajr al-Islam* (Cairo: Lajnat al-Ta'lif, 1945), p. 76; P. K. Hitti, *History of the Arabs* (London: Macmillan, 1946), p. 26; and E. G. Browne, A. *Literary History of Persia* (New York: Charles Scribner's Sons, 1902), pp. 189-91

2. Nicholson, *op. cit.,* p. 177.

3. "The believers are but Brethren, so make peace between your two brothers" (*The Koran*, ch. 49, verse 10).

4. A. Q. *al-Maghribi, Al-Akhlaq wa-al-Wajibat* (Cairo: Salafiyah Press, A.H. 1347), p. 128.

5. H. G. Wells, *The Outline of History* (New York: Garden City Publishing Co.,

1932), p. 268.

6. Hitti, *op. cit.*, p. 28.

7. The Students of Arab culture are usually perplexed as to whether Arab tribal people are democratic or aristocratic by nature. We believe that the Arabs are democratic and aristocratic at the same time. They are democratic within the tribe and aristocratic in the intertribal relationship.

8. *The Koran* also said, "Know that every Muslim is the brother of every Muslim. All of you are on the same level." (ch. 28, verse 29). Mohammed called the new social unit of loyalty "ummah," that is, congregation or community. Today, this term has lost its original meaning. It is now used by the Arabs to mean nation or nationality.

9. The five pillars of Islam are, in brief: (1) belief in the unity of Allah and in the prophethood of Mohammed; (2) prayer; (3) almsgiving; (4) fasting; and (5) pilgrimage.

10. *Asabiyah* also has been translated as a "group feeling," "feeling of unity," groupdom," "group mind," "social solidarity," "espirit de corps," "esprit de clan," and "tribal spirit." See S. Husari, *Dirasat an Muqaddimat Ibn Khaldun* (Beirut: Kashshaf Press, 1943), pp. 302-303; H. K. Sherwani, *Studies in Muslim Political Thought and Adminstration* (Lahore: Ashraf Press, 1963), p. 190; F. Rosenthal's introduction to his translation of Ibn Khaldun's *The Muqaddimah* (Princeton, N. J.: Princeton University Press, 1967), p. lxxviii; and H. Simon, *Ibn Khalduns Wissenschaft von der Menschlichen Kultur* (Leipzig, 1959), pp. 48, 57-61. *Asabiyah* can represent the social relationship within the tribal unit and also the loyalty of the tribe to its chief when he comes into contact or conflict with other chiefs. For details see T. Hussein, *Etude analytique et critique de la philosophie sociale d'Ibn-Khaldoun* (Paris: A. Pedone, 1917), p. 108; Y. Lacoste, *Ibn Khaldoun: naissance de l'histoire passé du tiers monde* (Arabic translation by M. Sulaiman, pp. 129-30); M. A. M. Nour, "Ibn Khaldun ka-Mufakir Ijtima'i Arabi," *A'mal Mahrajan Ibn Khaldun-1962* (Cairo: National Center for Social Research, 1962), p. 106; and Ch. Issawi, *An Arab Philosophy of History* (London: John Murray, 1950), pp. 10, 11.

11. See M. Abduh, ed. *Nahj al-Balaghah* (Cairo: Istiqamah Press, n.d.), vol. 2, pp. 173-74.

12. W. Muir, *Annals of the Early Caliphate* (London: Smith, Elder & Co., 1883), p. 61.

13. T. W. Arnold, *The Preaching of Islam,* (Lahore: Shirkat-i-Qualam, 1956), p. 28.

14. M. Khadduri, *The Law of War and Peace in Islam* (London: Luzac, 1940), pp. 4-5.

15. See *The Koran,* ch. 68, verses 51 and 52, and ch. 21, verse 107.

16. See Abd al-Rahman Ibn Khaldun, *Al-Muqaddimah* (Beirut: Dar al-Kashshaf, n.d.), p. 134.

17. A. Ibn Hanbal, *Musnad,* vol. 3, p. 425.

18. See *The Koran,* ch. 4, verse 40.

19. Hatim was well known in Arabia before Mohammed for his extreme generosity, hospitality, and good-will. He was considered by the Arabian nomads at the time as a representative of their ideals.

20. See Nicholson, *op. cit.*, pp. 86-87.

21. See Hitti, *op. cit.*, p. 128.

22. See al-Maghribi, *op. cit.*, p. 29.

23. Nicholson, *op. cit.*, p. 178.

24. See M. de Goeje, "Arabia," *Encyclopedia of Islam* (Leiden: Brill, 1913), vol. 1, p. 376; Nicholson, *op. cit.*, pp. 177-79; De Lacy O'Leary, *Arabia Before Muhammad* (New York: Dutton, 1927), p. 20; and Browne, *op. cit.*, pp. 187-89.

25. Nicholson, *op. cit.*, p. 179.

26. R. Levy, *An Introduction to the Sociology of Islam* (London: Williams and Norgate, 1931), vol. 1, p. 78.

27. Hitti, *op. cit.*, pp. 140-41.

28. Al-Tabari, *Tarikh,* vol. 3, p. 145, cited by D. Miqdadi, *Tarikh al-Ummat al-Arabiyah* (Baghdad: Ma'arif Press, 1932), p. 138.

29. Amin, *op. cit.*, pp. 146-47. Umar was the second caliph after the Prophet's death. He was, however, the adviser and the right hand of the first caliph, Abu Bakr, whose term lasted for a relatively short time. It is safe to conclude, therefore, that Umar was, more or less, the actual ruler of the Islamic state in its critical situation after the death of its founder.

30. Hitti, *op. cit.*, p. 29.

31. See J. Zaydan, *Tarikh al-Tamaddun al-Islami* (Cairo: Hilal Press, 1902), vol. 4, pp. 31-32, 34-35.

32. Ibn Khaldun, *Muqaddimah*, p. 130, also p. 126; and Zaydan, *op. cit.*, vol. 1, p. 14.

33. See, for example, Hitti, *op. cit.*, p. 27.

34. Cited by Nicholson, *op. cit.*, p. 190.

35. *Ibid.*, pp 189-90.

36. *Ibid.*, p. 190.

37. *Ibid.*

38. Ibn Khaldun, *Kitab al-Ibar,* vol. 3, pt. 1, pp. 140, 141.

39. See M. H. Zayn, *Al-Shi'ah fi al-Tarikh* (Saida: Irfan Press, 1938), p. 105.

40. M. Aqqad, *Abqariyat al-Imam* (Cairo: Ma'arif Press, 1952), pp. 27-73. See also Khadduri, *op. cit.*, p. 34.

41. Cited by Hitti, *op. cit.*, p. 25. See also P. K. Hitti, *The Arabs: A Short History.* (Chicago: Henry Regnery, 1956).

42. See G. L. Della Vida, "Umaiyad," *Encyclopedia of Islam,* vol. 4, p. 999. See also Nicholson, *op. cit.*, p. 191.

43. According to Ibn Khaldun, Mu'awiyah was merely a passive tool of the revived tribal spirit of the time. This, however, is not entirely true. Mu'awayah not only drifted with the revived tribal spirit, but also contributed to its revival.

44. Abu al-Hadid, *Sharh al-Nahj,* vol. 1, p. 180, cited by A. Amin. *Duha al-Islam* (Cairo: Lajnat al-Ta'lif, 1938), vol. 1, p. 23.

45. Amin, *Duha al-Islam,* vol. 1, pp. 23-24.

46. See Abduh, *op. cit.*, vol. 2, p. 103.

47. R. Strothmann, "Shia," *Encyclopedia of Islam* (Leiden: Brill, 1934), vol. 4, p. 353.

48. Zaydan, *op. cit.*, vol. 6, p. 58.

49. As a matter of fact, Ali was about to win in Siffin when his cunning rival

ordered his troops to raise copies of *The Koran* up on their spears and shout, "Let *The Koran* be the judge between us." Driven perhaps by a pious motive, Ali accepted the proposal and ordered his troops to stop fighting. The Seceders were in fact among those who influenced him to make the erroneous decision, which resulted finally in his defeat. Afterwards, they condemned him on account of this decision and his failure to win the war.

50. Amin, *Fajr al-Islam*, p. 261.

51. See Abduh, *op. cit.*, vol. 2, pp. 161ff.

52. Amin, *Fajr al-Islam*, pp. 262-63.

53. Nicholson, *op. cit.*, p. 211. See also Amin, *Duha al-Islam*, vol. 3, p. 334.

54. They flatly attributed their victory in the battle of Asak, where only forty of them defeated two thousand of their enemies, to the aid of Allah. See Amin, *Duha al-Islam*, vol. 3, pp. 343-44.

55. Amin, *Fajr al-Islam*, p. 262.

56. Della Vida, *op. cit.*, p. 998.

57. See Amin, *Duha al-Islam*, vol. 1, p. 23.

58. See Hussein, *op. cit.*, pp. 41-42.

59. See Ibn Khaldun, *Muqaddimah*, p. 543. It can be said that the nomadic man is naturally disposed toward poetry rather than toward science. Scientific discipline requires a more or less calm disposition to which the nomadic man is not ordinarily accustomed.

60. Al-Maghribi, *op. cit.*, pp. 49-55.

61. Cf. D. B. Macdonald, "'Ilm," *Encyclopedia of Islam* (Leiden: Brill, 1927), vol. 2, pp. 469-70.

62. Ibn Khaldun, *Muqaddimah*, p. 149. See also F. Baali's review of A. Wardi's *Dirasah fi Tabi'at al-Mujtama' al-Iraqi, American Sociological Review,* vol. 31 (December 1966), p. 883. Because of the secularization process at the present time this attitude is declining.

63. Ibn Khaldun, *Muqaddimah,* p. 394.

64. Hussein, *op. cit.*, pp. 195-96.

65. O'Leary, *loc.cit.*

66. Wells, *op. cit.*, p. 609.

67. As Simmel points out, "Depersonalization of authority relations makes subordination more tolerable and less humiliating." See R. Heberle "The Sociology of Georg Simmel: The Forms of Social Interaction," in H. E. Barnes, ed. *An Introduction to the History of Sociology* (Chicago: University of Chicago Press, 1948), p. 259.

68. D. de Santillana, "Law and Society," in T. Arnold and A. Guillaume, ed. *Legacy of Islam* (London: Oxford University Press, 1931), p. 286.

69. Y. Abu Yusuf, *Kitab al-Kharaj* (Cairo: Salafiyah Press, A. H. 1347), pp. 10-12.

70. Amin, *Fajr al-Islam*, pp. 67, 70.

71. A. Alayili, *Tarikh al-Husayn* (Beirut: Irfan Bookstore, n.d.) p. 81.

72. See A. H. Sharaf al-Din, *Al-Fusul al-Muhimmah* (Saida: Irfan Press, A. H. 1347), pp. 68-69. The orthodox historians may raise serious questions about the historical authenticity of this event; but, viewing it in the light of the fact that Umar was urging the Muslims to concentrate their attention and devotion to the war, one may be willing to accept it.

73. Alayili, *op. cit.*, pp. 89-90.

74. *Ibid.*, p. 87. See also Ibn Khaldun, *Muqaddimah*, p. 130.

75. Zaydan, *op. cit.*, vol. 4, pp. 31-32.

76. Cf. Ibn Khaldun, *Muqaddimah*, p. 131.

77. See Alayili, *op. cit.*, pp. 86-87.

78. Khadduri, *op. cit.*, p. 5.

79. *Ibid.*

80. For example, the Wahhabi and Sanusi movements.

81. The Khaldunian *asabiyah* has two aspects: political and social. The political aspects tends to attach members of a tribe to their leader—for example, in his conflict with other tribal leaders—while the social aspect unites members and helps them to form a well-integrated group. For details see Sherwani, *op. cit.*, p. 196; M. A. Enan, *Ibn Khaldun: His Life and Work* (Lahore: Ashraf Press, 1969), pp. 114, 170; and H. M. Rabi', *The Political Theory of Ibn Khaldun* (Leiden: E. J. Brill, 1967), p. 162 and also pp. 49, 65.

82. Ibn Khaldun, *Muqaddimah*, p. 175.

83. See Ibn Khaldun, *Muqaddimah*, p. 127.

84. *Ibid.*, p. 142.

85. *Ibid.*, pp. 142-43.

86. *Ibid.*, p. 148.

87. *Ibid.*, p. 150.

88. *Ibid.*, p. 540.

89. *Ibid.*, p. 142.

90. *Ibid.*, p. 372.

91. *Ibid.*, pp. 395-96. See also the English translation by Rosenthal, vol. 2, p. 344.

92. Ibn Khaldun, *Muqaddimah*, pp. 411-12, and also pp. 87-91; and Ibn Khaldun, *Kitab al-Ibar*, vol. 2, pt. 2 p. 111.

93. Ibn Khaldun, *Muqaddimah*, pp. 390-91.

94. In describing such a tendency among the orthodox writers in Islam, von Grunebaum says: "Depersonalization was favored by the moralist's habit of decomposing the human character into individual qualities, such as pride and humility, liberality and miserliness, truthfulness and dishonesty, which were discussed one after another, preferably in pairs of opposites." That is, the individual "was interesting merely as an illustration of a general observation which was owed to the sagacity of one of the wise." See G. E. von Grunebaum, *Medieval Islam* (Chicago: University of Chicago Press, 1946), pp. 225-26.

95. Ibn Khaldun, *Muqaddimah*, p. 151.

96. *Ibid.*, p. 150. O'Leary has a similar opinion about the Arabs before Islam. He believes that the Arab "sense of personal dignity is so strong that he is naturally in revolt against every form of authority... . A benefactor is a natural object of attack because a benefactor confers a sense of obligation, and consequently a sense of inferiority, upon the recipient of his generosity." (O'Leary, *op. cit.*, p. 20).

97. Ibn Khaldun, *Muqaddimah*, pp. 128-29. Here Ibn Khaldun appears to be influenced by the nomadic values. To him, the *asabiyah* is natural and universal. He does not realize that this also can be viewed through the relativistic perspective which he advocated and applied to many other aspects of social life. He believes, however, that a

blood relation is not necessary for the existence of the *asabiyah*. Man is naturally inclined to help his relatives. Whether the relation is true or false in reality does not matter in this regard; what actually matters is the social consideration. Ibn Khaldun regains at this point his usual sociological insight. The interpretation here is different from that of Ritter, Will, and Lahbabi (which places blood as the main source). See H. Ritter, "Irrational Solidarity Groups: A Socio-Psychological Study in Connection with Ibn Khaldun," *Oriens,* vol. 1 (1948), p. 19; M A. Lahbabi, *"Isalat al-Manhajiyah ind Ibn Khaldun,"* Mahrajan Ibn Khaldun (Casablanca: Dar El-Kitab, 1962), pp. 20-21; and E. Will's review of G. Nebel's *Sokrates in Revue Historique* (October-December 1970), p. 445.

98. Ibn Khaldun, *Muqaddimah*, pp. 149-52.

99. *Ibid.,* p. 151.

100. *Ibid.,* pp. 159-61.

101. Ibn Khaldun often relies on the traditions attributed to Umar, supporting his theory with the "sayings" and "doings" of Umar. This can be readily explained by the fact that, during the reign of Umar, Islam and Arabism, or religion and nomadism, were identical and synonymous. As regards Ali, the caliph who profoundly disliked the tribal spirit of the Arabian nomads and vehemently fought against it, Ibn Khaldun seems to be somewhat cold.

102. Essentially, there is no difference between the Judeo-Christian and Islamic attitudes toward city life. See, for example, P. A. Sorokin *et al. A Systematic Source Book in Rural Sociology* (Minneapolis, Minn.: University of Minnesota Press, 1930), vol. 1; and von Grunebaum, *op. cit.*, p. 174.

103. See Ibn Khaldun, *Muqaddimah*, pp. 123-24.

104. *Ibid.,* pp. 142, 394.

105. *Ibid.,* p. 128.

106. *Ibid.,* p. 203.

107. *The Koran,* ch. 49, verse 13.

108. Cited by Levy, *op. cit.*, p. 80.

109. Ibn Khaldun, *Muqaddimah,* p. 130. It should be emphasized that Ibn Khaldun also deals with economic factors in shaping nomadism and urbanism. To him, science and crafts have relative virtues. He explains science and crafts in terms of materialistic causes. They are usual in civilization, not because civilized people have brighter minds than others but because science and crafts are necessary products of civilized life, products that develop as a result of the interaction between supply and demand. In civilization the division of labor is so well developed that a great variety of economic goods is produced in quantities that are much more than necessary to satisfy the wants of civilized man. The surplus is used to satisfy luxurious wants. In nomadism, on the other hand, man endeavors to satisfy his basic wants; nomads are usually content with the bare means of subsistence. Although city dwellers have a higher standard of living, it is harmful for people, from the secular as well as the religious point of view, to live a luxurious life. Moreover, the urbanite's expenses oblige him to work hard and to seek money by every possible means. This eventually leads to moral disintegration and even to social disorganization. This is also true when the nomads become civilized; they begin to rely on the walls and the mercenary soldiers of the city for their defense and consequently lose their original *asabiyah,* bravery, and honor. They may become scientists, architects, or skilled craftsmen, but new skills and knowledge do not

compensate for the weakness in their manhood. Ibn Khaldun states that with few exceptions most "scientists" or scholars of Islam are non-Arabs, but he argues that this should not be interpreted as a weakness in the original nature of the Arabs. Due to their simple conditions the Arabs at the time of Mohammed had no sciences or crafts because there was no use for them. The oral transmission of *The Koran* and *hadith* (sayings of Mohammed) continued until the reign of Harun al-Rashid (d. 809). At that time, writing religious documents became a necessity. The Arabs left this and related studies "to the Persians and the mixed race which sprang from intermarriage of the conquerors with the conquered. They [the Arabs] did not entirely look down upon the men of learning but recognized their services, since after all it was Islam and the sciences connected with it that profited thereby" (Ibn Khaldun, *ibid.*, pp.122,361,371-74,400-401.543-44).

Chapter Two

RIGHT AND MIGHT: HISTORICAL PERSPECTIVE

The terms might and right* are used here in the social or relative sense. That is, they are collectively defined by members of a society. What is right in one society may not be so in another. Criteria of might or power may also change with a change of value systems.

The classic controversies over might versus right, politics versus religion, and realism versus idealism are meaningless in a sacred society. In such a society there is no gap between the so-called might and right. Among primitive peoples, men of power are usually the carriers of traditions. Thus it is difficult among these people to find despotic or unjust rulers. To use Pigors's term, the ruler in the sacred society is a "leader" rather than a "dominator."[1] He usually leads his people toward the goals they want, not the ones he himself wants. In short, there is no class exploitation or social injustice in the sacred society. The leader in such a society is usually the "father," the "shaikh," the "elder," or the like. He follows the same traditions, believes in the same mana, fears the same tabus, and worships the same "god" as his followers. To use Mead's terminology, he takes the role of the same "generalized other," that of his subjects. He looks through their eyes and feels the same as they feel.[2]

1.   *Right and Might in Islam*

Islam is a politico-religious phenomenon. Its founder, Mohammed, was in his latter years the sacred as well as the secular leader of the Muslim community. Many Western historians and orientalists, however, have criticized aspects of Mohammed's secular career. To quote Reynold Nicholson:

> Mohammed in the early part of his career presents a spectacle of
> grandeur which cannot fail to win our sympathy and admiration.
> At Medina . . . he appears in a less favorable light: the days of
> pure religious enthusiasm have passed away for ever, and the
> Prophet is overshadowedby the Statesman.[3]

Other writers attack Mohammed more severely.[4] It should be remembered that these writers view Mohammed from their own perspective; they impose the categories of their own culture on a man who experienced a quite different one. Most of them are Christians or living in a Christian environment where the dictum "Render therefore unto Caesar the things which are Caesar's, and unto God the things that are God's" is considered logical and natural. They probably have been taught since their early childhood that Jesus refused the "crown" offered to him, and so they tend to regard Mohammed as "a vulgar impostor" merely because he did accept a crown.[5] They thus overlook the radical difference between Jesus' society and that of Mohammed. In fact, Jesus lived in a secular society, where the gap between might and right was wide, whereas Mohammed lived in a nomadic society, where the sacred tribal association prevailed. As Toynbee reflects, "Muhammed did not happen to live under Caesar's jurisdiction... . This extreme difference of milieu explains, at least inpart, the extreme difference between the earthly fortunes of these two prophets."[6]

Toynbee's penetrating insight into the difference between the social milieus of Jesus and Mohammed falls short, however, of the more comprehensive explanation offered by sociology. Roman rule, which Toynbee emphasizes as the main difference between the two social milieus, does not cause the difference. Jesus could never have been a successful secular ruler, because the gap between religion and politics, between what ought to be and what is, was so wide in his society that no man on earth could really reconcile them. In nomadic Arabia, on the other hand, the society was, and still is, typically sacred. Its nucleus is a well-integrated tribe whose *shaikh* honestly serves its public interests.[7] Mohammed tried to be a Jesus-like prophet restricting himself to the purely sacred career, for about thirteen years to little avail. As Toynbee sums up the career: " As the result of thirteen years of propaganda, he had won no more than a handful of converts—most of whom had been compelled to fly the country."[8] Mohammed failed because the *Arabian nomads could not understand right without might behind it*. Most of the early converts were recruited from the slaves and the lower classes of the town.[9]

As soon as Mohammed changed, after the *Hijra* (migration to Medina), into a secular ruler and a successful commander in war, the Arabian nomads changed their attitude toward him. They began to regard him as a sacred prophet sent by Allah. "The victory itself," says Hitti, "was interpreted as a divine sanction of the new faith."[10] Commenting upon the battle of Badr,[11] in which Mohammed was victorious over his enemies, Nicholson says:

> Here, at last, was the miracle which the Prophet's enemies demaned
> of him... . The victory of Badr turned all eyes upon Muhammed. However
> little the Arabs cared for his religion, they could not but respect the man who
> had humbled the lords of Mecca. He was now a power in the land—
> "Muhammed, King of the Hijaz."In Medina his cause flourished mightily.
> The zealots were confirmed in their faith, the waverers convinced,
> the disaffected overawed.[12]

When Mohammed finally entered Mecca as a conqueror, his chief opponent, Abu Sufyan, declared his conversion to Islam, saying, "Oh, Mohammed, if our idols were real gods, they should have protected us from you."[13]

H. G. Wells severely criticizes Mohammed on the ground that he left his followers with no clear scheme for the orderly selection of his successors.[14] Abd al-Raziq, a modern Muslim writer, perhaps under Well's influence, sees Islam as a purely religious system; political entanglement is merely an incidental phenomenon not intended by the Prophet to be established upon a permanent basis. Because he was just a prophet and founder of a religion, not a king, Mohammed was completely right to neglect the question of succession after his death.[15] The difficulty with Wells and Abd al-Raziq is that they forgot that Mohammed was living in a sacred society in which the problem of electing the leader did not practically exist. Here again the writers impose the categories of their own society on a different one. It was not imperative, in fact, for Mohammed to plan a scheme of succession or election for a secular society which was not yet born.[16] Mohammed can be considered, in this regard, a *shaikh* rather than a king. The *shaikh* of a tribe does not worry at all about who is going to succeed him after his death. The successor will be chosen eventually for his own merits and his mana. True, the successor is sometimes required to be from the family of his predecessor, but this can be interpreted to indicate the possession of pure blood,[17] which ensures a powerful mana. The tribe may prefer the son of the old *shaikh,* believing that the *shaikh's* abilities have been inherited. Nevertheless, the succeeding son will be deposed from his office as soon as he loses his mana. In the words of Hitti, "His tenure of office lasts during the good-will of his constituency."[18]

When Mohammed died, the Muslims immediately hurried to elect his successor. They chose Abu Bakr, one of the most celebrated disciples of the Prophet. As a result, some disagreement and minor disturbances arose but no serious conflict developed. After the death of Abu Bakr, almost all the Muslims quietly submitted to his successor, Umar Ibn al-Khattab. There appeared no succession trouble because the Islamic society was still standing on its old foundation and had not yet come out from the sacred to the secular pattern. The gap between the upper and lower classes had not yet developed. In spite of his great integrity and wisdom, the second caliph Umar did something which in the opinion of some, caused a gap to develop. He began to distribute the spoils from the conquered countries, not equally as his predecessor had done, but unequally—to each according to his record of service and devotion to the cause of Islam.[19] This unequal distribution can be regarded as one of the factors leading to the rise of an aristocratic class in Islam. Umar himself became somewhat aware of the social consequences of the distribution of the spoils of war. When the extraordinary spoils from the Persian conquests came to Medina, he bitterly wept, saying to one of his intimate friends, "But Allah does not give this material treasure to a people without sowing at the same time the seeds of hostility and hatred among them."[20]   In fact, this prophecy of Umar came true shortly after his death.   Wide differences in wealth and prestige became established among the Muslims. The influence of social secularization gradually increased, particularly when the Muslims came into contact with the conquered civilizations and tried to adopt some of their luxuries and complex lifestyle.[21]

Unfortunately, the third caliph Uthman was weak and favored his relatives in the distribution of the spoils of war and in the appointment of officials.[22]   Uthman practiced, or was obliged to practice, an extreme nepotism in favor of men who were looked upon by the pious Muslims as "bad believers." In the words of Nicholson, "They soon climbed into all the most lucrative and important offices and lived on the fat of the land, while too often their ungodly behavior gave point to the question whether these converts of the eleventh hour were not still heathens at heart."[23]   As a result, two separate camps formed. One was led by Ali and some other pious companions of the Prophet, and the other camp was led by the Umayyads, the relatives of the aging caliph Uthman (who also happened to be the same men who had led the historical opposition of Mecca against Mohammed and who did not adopt Islam until Mecca was conquered.) One man who belonged to the pious camp deserves special note: Abu Dhar, who is considered by modern writers to be the prophet of socialism in Islam. Abu Dhar vehemently protested the big differences in wealth among the Muslims of his day. He preached that the rich should distribute their wealth among the poor and needy. After a long and severe struggle, he died in exile. The seed he had sown grew rapidly after his death, however. His tragic struggle and the continuous propaganda of the pious camp finally led to the murder of Uthman by an indignant mob.[24]

The pious camp temporarily triumphed with the election of Ali as Uthman's successor in the caliphate. The "idealistic" rule of Ali was destined to last a very short time. The lower classes which had supported Ali in this election were too weak to prevent the "realistic" tide from rising. Mu'awiyah led the opposition against Ali and eventually defeated him.

During the Umayyad dynasty, which was founded by Muawiyah, the contrast between what Wells calls the palace and the temple was very clear. The name of Ali became at that time the standard under which the camp of "right" gathered, while the camp of "might" gathered around the triumphant Umayyads.[25]

It is interesting to note that most of the Arabs sided with the Umayyads, while the non-Arabs sided against them.[26] Looking at the phenomenon from the perspective established in the present chapter, however, we can say that the reason does not lie in the Arabs' lack of religious sincerity, as some modern students of Islam have thought. It lies rather in the fact that the Arabs were at that time mostly nomadic in their cultural outlook and social values. They looked at might and right from what has been referred to in this book as the primitive perspective. When the Umayyads defeated Ali and established their victorious dynasty the Arabs saw this as a clear sign that right was siding with the Umayyads. This will be more clearly understood if we remember that the Umayyads respected the nomadic folkways and mores more than they respected those of Islam.[27] Moreover, they enlarged the area of the Islamic Empire to an astonishing extent. The greatest of the Islamic conquests took place under their regime.[28] The armies which helped to achieve such a "miraculous" victory and enjoyed its booty were mostly recruited from among the Arabs themselves. Mu'awiyah himself declared once, from the pulpit of the mosque, that his victory over Ali was indubitable proof of his "righteousness" in the sight of Allah.[29] He might not have actually believed that, but to declare it from the pulpit of the mosque indicated his faith in his audience's credulity.

At any rate, the Arabs began under the leadership of the Umayyads to develop a deep contempt for the non-Arab Muslims. Mu'awiyah is once reported to have said:

> I notice that these reds (the non-Arab Moslems) have increased in Number... . I imagine they will, someday, rebel against the Arabs and the government, and so I have an intention to kill part of them and leave the other part enslaved for the purpose of establishing markets and building roads. [30]

As a reaction against this discrimination, the non-Arab Muslims resorted to the study of the sacred Traditions of Mohammed and his Rashidin caliphs. The mosques then became schools for learning and the newly rising "sciences" of Islam, and many "scientists" were, as Ibn Khaldun points out, non-Arab.[31]

Hence, the Muslims were divided into two separate groups: soldiers and scientists, followers of might and followers of right. The Arabs represented the conquerors, who believed that the sword was the final judge in the world, whereas the non-Arabs represented the conquered, who resorted to the realm of ideas and ideals, or what Nietzsche called "transvaluation," as a protest against the severe judgment of the sword. Consequently, the contrast between the temple and the palace, or in this case the mosque and the *qasr,* became obvious.

2.   *Millennial Hope*

Islam was, and still is, full of the millennial hope which usually goes under the name of Mahdism.[32] It seems natural for Muslims to wait for the expected savior (Mahdi), since they often feel a wide discrepancy between the ideal principles of Mohammed and the actual conditions of their politico-religious life.[33]

Modern students of Islam believe that the idea of the Mahdi was developed in Islam during the Umayyad period under the influence of Jewish and Christian Messianism and then was attributed to the *hadith* (sayings of Mohammed).[34] Some modern students of Islam believe that Mohammed was not interested in a millennial hope because he was a victorious prophet. They seem to see little reason for Mohammed to prophesy about a "future savior," since he considered himself the "future savior" of his people; and he actually achieved what was expected of him in this respect. Here again, we notice that scholars impose their own presuppositions and categories of thought on others. In fact, there was good reason for Mohammed to be interested in the Millennial hope, especially in the first period of his prophetic mission when he was helplessly and hopelessly striving against overwhelming forces. Mohammed was not victorious at the beginning of his mission. In the first period of the mission, he was, in some sense, a prophet of the biblical type; he was greatly influenced by Judaeo-Christian attitudinal-complex.[35] It is natural, therefore, to find that Mohammed shows the same interest in Messianism as the Jews and the Christians did before him. Unfortunately, modern students of Islam usually overlook the fact that Mohammed was an admirer of the Hebrew prophets and tried to follow their footsteps as far as possible.[36]

The word Mahdi was unknown in Arabia before Mohammed, a fact that has led modern students of Islam to wonder about its origin. Mohammed probably developed the word Mahdi just to be the Arabic equivalent of the Hebrew term of Messiah. Both have almost the same meaning; whereas Messiah means the anointed one, Mahdi means "the divinely guided one."[37] The faithful believe that the Mahdi, like the Messiah, will appear in some future time to deliver them from the prevailing social injustices. The fact that he will be "divinely guided," or "anointed," assures that in his person might and right will be combined again.

The Mohammedan Traditions often mention the coming of Jesus along with the rise of the Mahdi. The two deliverers will, according to the Traditions, cooperate in the fight against the anti-Christ, or *al-Masih al-Dajjal*[38] as the Traditions call him. Macdonald states, "But in this development [of the Mahdi tradition] the roles assigned to Jesus and to the Mahdi came to be confusingly alike, and one party tried to cut the knot with a Tradition from Muhammad. 'There is no Mahdi save Isa B. Maryam'."[39] This tradition declaring that there is no Mahdi save Jesus has long troubled the minds of Muslim Traditionists.[40] What did the Prophet really mean by that? The Traditionists differ widely in answering this perplexing question. It appears that Mohammed meant what he said: there is no Mahdi save Jesus. This should be clearly understood if we remember that late in his life Mohammed developed an intense dislike for the pride and arrogance of the Jews.[41] We can find, moreover, some verses in *The Koran* which obviously indicate that Mohammed sided with the Christians against the Jews.[42]   From this perspective, we may be able to see in the aforementioned Tradition, which identifies the Mahdi with Jesus, an indirect challenge by Mohammed to the Jews.

Mahdism seems gradually to have lost its grip upon the minds of the Muslims after they became victorious and began to build their huge empire. The hope of the early days began to die out as a result of the rising might of Islam. During the Rashidin period, might and right appeared to go hand in hand. The Mahdi was then not wanted; Muslims put aside the idea of the future deliverer for later days. Even when Mu'awiyah defeated Ali and set the "unorthodox" dynasty of the Umayyads on the throne of the caliphate, no Mahdi was in sight. The pious Muslims still believed that the right kind of government would sooner or later be restored. The first Mahdi in Islam, however, as history tells us, appeared immediately after the murder of Husayn, the grandson of Mohammed, at the hands of an Umayyad army.[43]   This Mahdi was Ibn al-Hanafiyah, a half-brother of Husayn. It seems that Ibn al-Hanafiyah did not actually want to be called Mahdi. Some Muslims were perhaps so depressed by Husayn's murder that they could not refrain from reviving the long-dormant tradition of the Mahdi. When Ibn al-Hanafiyah died, his followers believed that he had not actually died. He was, they said, merely retiring from this evil world to live somewhere in the mountains outside the Medina, waiting for the order of Allah to come out to deliver his people from the prevailing social injustice.[44]

During the Umayyad period, and the Abbasid period afterwards, many Mahdis arose. Almost all of them were Alids,[45] that is, descendants of Ali. The name of Ali was, as we have seen before, a pregnant symbol of protest against the secularization of the caliphate. Thus we find the terms Alid or Fatimid[46] often associated with the name Mahdi. In fact, most of the Traditions of the Mahdi usually attributed to the Prophet indicate this association.[47]   This led Amin to conclude that the idea of the Mahdi is a Shiite invention. Moreover, he attributes the spread of the idea among the orthodox Muslims to the work of the Sufites, who adopted it from the Shiites.[48]   Amin overlooks the fact that *Mahdism is a kind of millennial hope, or messianism, that can be found, in one form or another, in almost all societies in which might and right are thought to be in conflict.* To quote Kohn:

> Messianism is never mere theoretical speculation about things to come;
> it is always a living practical force. It is a belief held with religious
> fervor by oppressed or unfortunate groups (ethnic, social, religious) or
> by men suffering either from the imperfection of their fellow human beings
> or from the consciousness of their own inadequacy, that a change will come
> which will end their sufferings and fill the world with piety and justice.
> There is always in messianism a non-acceptance of the present order and
> a sentiment of revolt against things which seem unbearable.[49]

The Shiites, it is true, were the first Islamic group who seriously believed in the Mahdi. They did so mainly because they were the first group in Islam who felt the burden of injustice under the Umayyad caliphate. The Umayyads in fact used every means possible to suppress Shiism and to blemish the name of Ali, which was considered the seed of Shiism.[50] Afterwards, the Sufites adopted Mahdism. Sufism is a kind of mysticism developed in Islam as a protest against the profanation of the caliphate and the moral disintegration of Islamic society.[51] Following von Wiese's theoretical explanation, we can regard Sufism as the "cult" and Shiism as the "sect" of Islam. In his opinion, both of these two ideal types, the cult and the sect, usually rise against the secularization of religion or the adulteration of its old ideals.[52]

There is a significant difference, however, between the Mahdi of the Shiites and that of the Sufites, and it penetrated finally into the whole body of Islam. The Shiites believe that the Mahdi is a historical man who lived once in the past and then disappeared and retired to a place beyond the reach of ordinary persons. He is awaiting the order of Allah to appear and "fill the earth with justice after it has been full of injustice." That is, he will not die until he appears again in this world and fulfills his mission.[53] The Sufites, on the other hand, believe that the Mahdi is an ordinary man; he will be born someday in the future, and after he reaches the age of maturity he will rise to achieve his mission of social delivery. Hence we have seldom seen a Mahdi rise among the Shiites. This may be due to the supernatural and supranatural   qualities they attribute to his life and his past career.

Among the orthodox Muslim groups the doctrine of Mahdism is a dynamic social factor. It produced, and is still producing, many uprisings, upheavals, and social movements in Islamic society. To the orthodox masses, the Mahdi is an ordinary man; any man with a prophetic tendency may feel that he is the expected deliverer of Islam. Thus Mahdism became one of the few doctrines that saved Islamic society from complete stagnation during its dark ages.[54]

NOTES

* In association with A. Wardi.

1. P. Pigors, *Ledership and Domination* (New York: Houghton Mifflin, 1935), passim.

2. G. H. Mead, *Mind, Self and Society* (Chicago: University of Chicago Press, 1934), pp. 152-164. See also W. Durant, *The Story of Civilization* (New York: Simon and Schuster, 1942), pp. 23-25.

3. R. A. Nicholson, *A Literary History of the Arabs* (Cambridge: University Press, 1930), p. 169.

4. For more information see A. J. Toynbee, *A Study of History* (New York:

Oxford University Press, 1962), vol. 3, pp. 468-69; H. G. Wells, *Outline of History* (New York: Garden City Publishing Co., 1932), pp. 607-608; and J. Schacht, "Mohammed," *Encyclopedia of Social Sciences,* 1931, vol. 10, p. 570.

5. "In quarters hostile to Islam and to its founder, this 'worldliness' has been a popular object of denunciation" (Toynbee, *op. cit.,* p. 468).

6. *Ibid.,* p. 469.

7. P. K. Hitti, *History of the Arabs* (London: Macmillan, 1946), pp. 26-28.

8. Toynbee, *loc. cit.*

9. See S. Lane-Poole, *The Speeches and Table-Talk of the Prophet Mohammed* (London: Macmillan, 1905), p. xxxiii; H. Masse, *Islam* (New York: Putnam, 1938), p. 37; R. Levy, *An Introduction to the Sociology of Islam* (London: Williams and Norgate, 1931), vol. 1, p. 77; Nicholson, *op. cit.,* p. 154; and Hitti, *op. cit.,* p. 133. It should be mentioned here that Mecca alone, in contrast to all of its neighboring communities, fell under some sort of secularization process because of its brisk commercial activities. There appeared, therefore, certain individuals who felt the oppression of the secularization process and so were attracted, as Nicholson *(loc. cit.)* points out, by the leveling ideas of Islam.

10. Hitti, *op. cit.,* p. 117.

11. See *The Koran,* ch. 3, verse 11.

12. Nicholson, *op. cit.,* pp. 174-75.

13. This well-known saying, attributed to the archenemy of Mohammed at his conversion to the religion of Islam, clearly indicates the popular belief that might is necessarily associated with right. Cf. A. J. Sahhar, *Ahl al-Bayt* (Cairo: Misr Press, 1968), pp. 25, 27.

14. Wells, *op. cit.,* p. 622.

15. A. Abd al-Raziq, *Al-Islam wa Usul al-Hukm* (Cairo: Misr Press, 1925), pp. 93-95 and *passim.*

16. Ibn Khaldun also believes in the unimportance of appointing a successor at the time of the Prophet's death (*Muqaddimah,* p. 213). There is some well-supported evidence indicating that Mohammed had tried repeatedly to appoint Ali, his favorite cousin and son-in-law, as his successor. It seems that the objection against this appointment raised by some of his influential companions had finally caused him to drop it. See A. Ali, *Spirit of Islam* (London: Christophers, 1949), p. 431; D. M. Donaldson, *Aqidat al-Shi'a* (Cairo: Sa'ada Press, 1933), pp. 22-27, 60; A. Aqqad, *Abqariyat al-Imam* (Cairo: Ma'arif Press), pp. 165-67; and Ibn Khaldun, *Muqaddimah,* p. 212.

17. The Arabian nomads pay great attention to blood relationship. See W. R. Smith, *Kinship and Marriage in Early Arabia* (London: Adam & Black, 1903), pp. 26, 46. In fact, no other group in the world is as careful about the purity of its blood and its long pedigree as the Arabs. See Hitti, *op. cit.,* p. 28. They even guard the blood purity of their horses.

18. Hitti, *loc. cit.*

20. *Ibid.,* p. 56.

21. See Ibn Khaldun, *Muqaddimah,* pp. 204-205.

22. See, for example, A. Gilman, *Story of the Saracens from the Earliest Times to the Fall of Baghdad* (New York: Putnam's Sons, 1887), p. 266.

23. Nicholson, *op. cit.,* p. 190.

24. A. al-Subayti, *Abu Dhar* (Tehran: Sa'adi Press, 1945). Abu Dhar was the only nomadic person among the Prophet's companions. This may explain his extreme vehemence against the inequality of wealth which developed after the death of his beloved master, Mohammed.

25. Cf. J. Schacht, "Usul," *Encyclopedia of Islam* (Leiden: Brill, 1934), vol. 4, p. 1055.

26. A. Amin, *Duha al-Islam* (Cairo: Lajnat al-Ta'lif, 1938), vol. 1. pp. 32-33.

27. G. L. Della Vida, "Umaiyad," *Encyclopedia of Islam,* 1934, vol. 4, pp. 998-99. According to Macdonald, the Umayyad dynasty "was in many ways a return to pre-Muslim times and to an easy enjoyment of worldly things; it was a rejection of the yoke of Muhammad in all but form and name." See D. B. Macdonald, *The Development of Muslim Theology, Jurisprudence, and Constitutional Theory* (New York: Charles Scribner's Sons, 1903) p. 131.

28. See, for example, D. Miqdadi, *Tarikh al-Ummah al-Arabiyah* (Baghdad: Ma'arif Press, 1932), pp. 233-37.

29. See, for example, Sahhar, *op. cit.,* pp. 227, 260, 324.

30. Cited by A. Amin, *Fajr al-Islam* (Cairo: Lajnat al-Ta'lif, 1945), p.90.

31. Ibn Khaldun, *Muqaddimah,* pp. 543-45.

32. In Islam, the millennial hope or Mahdism has been the refuge from injustice.

33. See J. Schacht, "Sharia," *Encyclopedia of Islam,* 1934, vol. 4, p. 323.

34. See H. Kohn, "Messianism," *Encyclopedia of Social Sciences,* 1931, vol. 10, p. 363; D. S. Margoliouth, "Mahdi," *Encyclopedia of Religion and Ethics,* 1908, vol. 8, pp. 336-40; and D. M. Donaldson, *op. cit.,* 230-31.

35. Hitti, *op.cit.,* p. 468. See also Toynbee, op. cit., p. 468.

36. Almost all the historical narratives of *The Koran* have their biblical parallels.

37. This seems to be the most acceptable interpretation of the term Mahdi. See Margoliouth, *op. cit.,* p. 336; and P. K. Hitti, *Makers of Arab History* (New York: Harper, 1968), p. 96.

38. The "Masih al-Dajjal" means in Arabic the "False Messiah." See A. J. Wensinck, "Masih," *Encyclopedia of Islam* (Leiden: Brill, 1936), vol. 3, p. 391; B. Carra de Vaux, "Dadjjal," *Encyclopedia of Islam* (Leiden" Brill, 1913), vol. 1, p. 887; and D. M. Donaldson, *op. cit.,* pp. 242-43.

39. D. B. Macdonald, "Isa," *Encyclopedia of Islam* (Leiden: Brill, 1927), vol. 2, p. 525. "'Isa Ibn Maryam" means "Jesus, the son of Mary."

40. Ibn Khaldun, *Muqaddimah,* pp. 322, 325, 327.

41. H. Speyer, "Yahud," *Encyclopedia of Islam,* 1934, vol. 4, p. 1148.

42. *The Koran* says, "You will meet no greater enemy of the believers than the Jews and the Heathens and more inclined to friendliness to believers than those who say, 'We are Christians,' for there are priests and monks among them and they are not arrogant," ch. 5, verse 85. See also the *Meaning of the Glorious Koran,* trans. by Mohammed Marmaduke Pickthall (New York: New American Library), ch. 5, verse 82.

43. See Margoliouth, *loc. cit.;* Amin, *Duha al-Islam,* vol. 3, p. 236; and Donaldson, *op. cit.,* p. 231. Mohammed is known to have loved his grandchild Husayn a great deal. There are several traditional sayings attributed to Mohammed denoting the high position of Husayn in his eyes. When Husayn was brutally killed with his family and

followers by the Ummayad army, the pious Muslims were enormously shocked. This may explain why the first Mahdi in Islam appeared after his murder.

44. Amin, *Duha al-Islam,* vol. 3, pp. 236-37.

45. Margoliouth, *op. cit.,* pp. 336-37.

46. Fatimid means a descendant of Fatimah the daughter of Mohammed and the wife of Ali. Hence, Fatimid and Alid are sometimes used synonymously.

47. See Ibn Khaldun, *Muqaddimah,* pt. 3, ch. 52, passim.

48. Amin, *Duha al-Islam,* vol. 3, pp. 236-46. The Shiites are the partisans of Ali.

49. Kohn, *op. cit.,* vol. 10, p. 357.

50. Abu al-Hadid, *Sharh al-Nahi,* vol. 1, pp. 356, 358, 359, and vol. 3, p. 15. Cited by M. H. Zayn, *Al-Shi'ah fi-alTurikh* (Saida: Irfan Press, 1938), p. 24.

51. See E. G. Browne, A Literary History of Persia (Cambridge: University Press, 1969), vol. 1, p. 416; and A. Amin, Zuhr al-Islam (Cairo: Lajnat al-Ta'lif, 1945), vol. 1, p. 121.

52. See L. von Wiese, *Systematic Sociology* (New York: Arno Press, 1974), ch. 44. The only difference between the cult and the sect in this respect lies in the fact that the former is an individual reaction whereas the latter is a social one.

53. Donaldson, *op. cit.,* ch. 21, passim.

54. Amin believes that Mahdism was, on the contrary, a sort of opium to the masses. In his own words, "the ruler becomes corrupt while the masses dream" (*Duha al-Islam,* vol. 3, p. 246). On p. 244 in the same volume, however, Amin attributes many of the revolutions and social upheavals, especially in the West, to the idea of Mahdism.

Chapter 3

ARAB UNITY AND DISUNITY IN MODERN TIME

As the Islamic-Arabic civilization and power declined, the Arabs and Muslims found themselves encircled and attacked from three different fronts at almost the same time. The Mongols had attacked from the east, the Crusaders from the north, and the Spaniards from the west. The Arabs and Muslims were helplessly defending their lands and wondering what had caused all these deadly troubles.

It was only in the past 100 years that the Arabs began to assert their identity and their right for a unity of its members. This aspiration was triggered, to some extent, by the Ottoman occupation of the Arab lands, by the oppression under the ruler Abdul-Hameed, and by the discriminatory policies of the Young Turks. Detecting the Arab aspiration for self-determination, the British government initiated negotiations with Sharif Hussain, who acted on behalf of the Arabs. In 1915-1916, Hussain specified the demands of Arab nationalists and, accordingly, an agreement was "concluded with the British government, bore the stamp of approval of those nationalist leaders."[1]

Soon after the conclusion of the British-Arab negotiations, "the British government started secret conversations with the French to decide how the Fertile Crescent of Iraq and Greater Syria should be divided between Britain and France."[2] This (Sykes-Picot Agreement), according to Nutting, was shameful.[3] No sooner had the betrayal of the Arab cause became a reality, than the British government prepared to betray the Arabs again through the Balfour Declaration of November 1917, "pledging British support for a 'national home' for the Jews in Palestine."[4] To add insult to injury, and in order "to calm Arabs suspicions [sic]", the British government in March 1918 sent out the leader of the Zionist movement "to Cairo and Jerusalem to reassure Arab leaders in Egypt and Palestine that Zionist plans for Jewish migration to Palestine would not prejudice Arab right."[5]

1.   *Arab Unity*

The Balfour Declaration, "the cynical betrayal of the Arab cause by Britain and France through the Sykes-Picot Agreement,"[6] and "the fragmentation of the Arab nationalist movement," especially in Lebanon and Palestine, were setbacks that implicitly paved the path for a movement toward unity. Arab unity, then, "had been conceived in four turbulent years which intervened between the Armistice of 1918 and the final imposition of the post-war settlement in 1922."[7] Through nationalism, the Arab people sought and are still seeking, "to reconstruct the foundations of their life, after centuries of suspended animation."[8] By the end of the 1930's, "the idea of Arab unity had journeyed toward its final form. It had come to rest in the doctrine which at that time enjoyed wide acceptance among the Arabs—*the doctrine of an Arab nation –in-being*."[9]

2.   *Determinants of Arab Unity*
     Now, questions can be raised: what does an Arab nation mean today? What are the elements of nationalism and, for that matter, Arab unity? And, what roles do the Muslim and Christian Arabs play in the formation of Arab unity?
     According to Sayegh, there was a unanimous agreement that "*language, culture,* and *history* among Arabs had contributed to the formation of the Arab nation, and now marked the Arabs and distinguished them as a nation from others."[10]   He acknowledges two more determinants: the uninterrupted geographical continuity (from Mauritania and Morocco to Iraq), and "the subjective factors of *consciousness* and volition--normally, the awareness of Arabs that they were Arabs."[11]   Language is ranked first as a major determinant. This is because, as Nuseibah points out, "it is the medium through which a people express their minds and motions."[12] In analyzing the factor of language, Zurayq was convinced that every language possesses unique attributes which distinguish it from other languages.   "The Arab language among all other languages has shown great vitality in its meticulous structure, the extent of its dissemination, and its flexibility, which has fitted it to serve as an efficacious instrument for expressing the various arts and sciences." As a result, "it behooves us to try to discover the secret of this vitality and to lay our hands on the unique powers which our language represents in order to utilize these powers in organizing our present and building our future."[13]

     Tutsch also believes that "of all elements of Arab unity language remains the strongest. Its importance as an integrating factor in the Arab world is stressed by every writer, every politician."[14]

     As for history, Nicholas Ziyadeh, Yusef Haykal, and Nabih Faris, among others, give to this determinant "an influence second only to that of language," whereas Zurayq places history "in the third place, i.e., after language and culture."[15]

     National consciousness, as a determinant of Arab unity received great attention from Zurayq, e.g., his analysis of historical consciousness as an integral part of national consciousness. He believes that "it is of utmost importance that we understand the basic factors which have contributed to our past greatness as well as to our retrenchment." It is also important to keep in mind "how many nations have collapsed, seemingly at the hands of foreign conquerors, while in fact they had already disintegrated from within prior to any onslaught from without."[16]

Another determinant was also added: "common Arab concerns and interests." Although this one is embedded in the concepts of national consciousness, history, and culture, Patai indicated that "the word 'Arab' has an almost magic power ... news about Arabs in trouble, even thousands of miles away, can easily provoke them to violent manifestations of solidarity."[17]   He continued:

> That the Arabs are brothers is for them axiomatic, a tenet of faith which,
> like other credos, neither requires proofs nor is capable of being refuted
> or even as much as shaken by specific instances of Arab disunity, or
> fratricidal wars, or other manifestations of Arab dissention, strife, or enmity.[18]

The Religion Factor: Does Arab unity reject pan-Islamism as an extreme movement lacking realistic vision?   Arab unity as a concept, as an ideology, or as a concrete reality, does not exclude Muslims since they constitute the majority of the Arab population, nor does it ignore the Christian Arab minority which shares the same language, culture, history, contiguous territory, and consciousness of kind.   Zurayq defines nation as a "group of people who have lived together over a long period of time, and whose national edifice is reinforced by language, a common homeland, economic life, culture, customs and traditions."[19]   Zurayq adds:

> True nationalism can in no case be incompatible with true religion,
> because in its essence it is naught by a spiritual movement which aims
> at the regeneration of the inner forces of a nation and the realization of
> its mental and spiritual potentialities. Nationalism, being a spiritual
> movement, must go hand in hand with religion and derive from it strength
> and life. Such is the case with Arab nationalism in its true sense: it
> neither opposes nor contradicts any religion, but accepts them all.
> If nationalism is opposed to anything, it is not to religious spirituality,
> but to the disruptive partisanship which places communal solidarity above
> the bonds of nationality and which refuses to be assimilated within
> the framework of the nation. The upholders of his partisanship are the
> enemies of Arab nationalism and the destroyers of its unity. As for true
> religion, it emanates, with nationalism, from the same spring.[20]

It should be realized that Arabism and Islamism are not identical. Indeed Islam appeared in Arabia, but, in addition to theology, it embraces principles of socio-political aspects of life and can be considered "a potent element of Arabism and a unifying factor in Arab society; and as such, Islam is a partial determinant of Arab nationhood."[21]

Although Islam is officially the state religion in the Arab world (with the exception of Lebanon where traditionally Christians constitute a majority), it is a politico-religious system. It differs from most of the religions of the world in that its founder was a secular ruler as well as a religious leader. This combination of religion and politics was quite easy and natural at the time of Mohammed.

Coming back to Christian Arabs, Sayegh believes that the Arab national movement "reflects the aspiration of Arabs of *all* faiths to establish a secular Arab society consolidated by the community of language, culture, history, and territory, and animated by a desire for *national* freedom, political unity, and human progress of which *all* Arabs will be beneficiaries and for the attainment of which *all* Arabs have struggled and will struggle, regardless of their faith."[22] Tutsch agrees: "Secularism tends to abolish the religious barrier between different Islamic groups and between the various religions."[23] In fact, Husari claims that "nationalism is strictly secular movement which has nothing to do with religion."[24]

Although demographically speaking, the Christians constitute a minority, their significant contribution to Arab nationalist movement cannot be ignored. However, "diffidence and ambiguity have kept important sections of the Christian Arabs lukewarm and suspicious, for they fear, with some justification, that Arab nationalism without a more forthright reorientation along secular lines may be no more than a façade for an Islamic policy, to which they naturally could not subscribe."[25] Zuraiq, one of the main proponents of Arab nationalism, and Albert Hourani, a well-known scholar, both Christian, affirmed their belief that " a certain Islamic element would always remain important in that combination of ideas which make up the popular nationalism."[26]

3.   *Efforts Toward Arab Unity*
As we have stated, Zuraiq and other proponents of Arab nationalism believe that for their unity the Arab share certain elements or determinants in common, e.g., language, culture (including shared interests), history, and contiguous territory. A solid unity should provide the Arabs with the needed democracy and "a greater sense of solidarity vis-à-vis the outside world."[27] Sayegh adds:

> In the free, unhindered advance towards Arab unity... lies the only hope
> for *moderate, orderly,* and *peaceful* progress towards the attainment of
> the human aspirations of the Arab peoples for the exercise of their God-given
> rights to liberty, solidarity, and a more abundant life.[28]

For many Arabs today, Arab unity is a predetermined aspect of their political life; it is beyond resistibility. "Hindered and retarded it may be – but

not indefinitely arrested."[29]

The first formal Arab unity in modern time, The United Arab Republic, was proclaimed on February 1, 1958, between Egypt and Syria. The constitution of this union was promulgated in March of 1958. Arab public opinion "greeted the union with happy excitement, not from what it was in itself, but also and perhaps primarily for the promise it held for eventual unification of the Arab World in its entirety ... ."[30]

Soon after, the Federation of the Arab State of North Africa (al-Maghrib al-Arabi) and the federation of Iraq and Jordan were formed. The latter "was obviously prompted, at least in part, by a desire to counteract the tremendous psychological effect which the proclamation of the United Arab Republic had upon the minds of the populations of Iraq and Jordan, eager as they were for Arab unity."[31] It seems that the July 1958 revolution in Iraq did not encourage Baghdad to join the United Arab Republic. One may be able to detect Iraq's preference for federation, not unity, in its leader's speech on June 15, 1962: "the Iraqi flag will fly in Iraq and the Syrian flag will fly in Syria. But the frontiers between us will disappear, for we are one people and one country."[32] Within a few months, all of these "unity," "federation," and "union" among the Arab states were dissolved. Local, instead of Pan-Arab nationalism began to surface again, the most conspicuous example of which was the Lebanese nationalism. From the 1970's until present today, one can witness more inter-governmental clashes, differences, and hostilities than ever before. Cultural, especially educational, cooperation continues to be somewhat strong.

4.   *Arab Disunity*

There are several inherent weaknesses of the idea of Arab unity. Sayegh specified three: its vagueness as to form, including "general indifference to instruments and methods; its oblivion to disunifying political forces; and its scorn for utilitarian inducements." They might reflect "an imbalance in the Arab outlook on socio-political affairs."[33]   Another weakness is manifested in "the failure of the exponents of the idea of Arab unity to take due cognizance of the real, objective, and stubborn elements of *diversity* in the Arab World." The Arab situation was to some extent ignored, by adopting the European concept of nationalism which evolved "within a concrete European context" and which "was bound to engender many of the ideological paradoxes which bedeviled Arab nationalist thought."[34]   More specific factors that have contributed to the weakness of the Arab unity movement are:

1. *The ineffectiveness of the Arab League:* The establishment of the League of Arab States in 1945 was not for Arab unity at all. Rather, it was merely "to coordinate the policies and measures of its member-states, whose sovereignty was to be preserved intact within the loose structure of the League."

That is, "at the hands officialdom the idea of unity took a different shape from that envisaged by the public. Representatives of governments ... were sensitive to, and were swayed by, the push and pull of discordant governmental interests, inter-governmental rivalries, and mutual suspicions."[35]   For instance, the Kingdom of Egypt was more concerned with preserving the "unity" of the Nile Valley, which can be considered an isolationist attempt.

Thus, meetings of the Arab League, including summit meetings, have been characterized by conflict. In fact "it was impossible for the Arab heads of states to convene a summit between 1990 and 1996 – a period of enormous change in the regional system."[36]   Nutting believes that "the Arab League *failed* to save Palestine from being engulfed by Israelis."[37] Even the "coordination" of efforts by the Arab League has failed to embrace the Palestinian *intifadas* (uprisings) against Israeli occupation of Palestinian lands.

2. *Inter-Arab disputes and rivalries:* The Arab inter-governmental relations continue to be marred by bickering, mistrust, mutual suspicions, and even deception. Those differences are not peripheral; they are becoming more potent and more conspicuous as disintegrative factors. "They explain why integration has not been forthcoming and why cooperation has been and probably will remain bumpy."[38]

In the Arab East, Lebanon experienced a decade of civil war that began in 1975. Similar events occurred also in Sudan and Somalia. These countries suffered, among other things, serious economic problems. In the Persian Gulf region, Iraq waged an eight-year war (1980-1988) against neighboring Iran. Two years later, Iraq invaded Kuwait. This invasion, which led Iraq to fight Arab countries, is regarded by some analysts as marking "the final collapse of the Arab unity project."[39] Additional consequences: More than one decade of severe sanctions against Iraq, a situation that added more suffering among the Iraqi people and left their economy in shambles. It was followed by the United States pre-emptive war on Iraq. Also in this region was the "controversy in 1997 over Qatar's decision to host the fourth annual Middle East regional economic meeting, with Israel in attendance, at a moment when the Arab-Israeli preace process was in a state of acute crisis."[40]

The Arab West (the Maghrib of North Africa) also witnessed some ups and downs of inter-Arab relations. Although the purpose of the formation of the Maghrib Union (UMA) is to foster cooperation and integration, rivalries between Morocco and Algeria, "Libyan interference, Tunisian mediation, and Mauritanian vulnerability ... continue to dominate the region, tearing unity apart."[41]   Moreover, after several meetings in late 2003, the representatives of these states failed to reach a unifying position.

What we are observing in the Arab world today is, to a large extent, a narrow *asabiyah* (solidarity, unity) which emphasizes loyalty to a tribe, to a locality (Lebanon, Saudi Arabia), to a religious group (Muslim, Christian), to a specific Islamic sect (Shiite, Sunnite or even Wahabi), and to a particular Christian church (Maronite, Eastern Catholic).

3. *Scientific and Technological Underdevelopment:* Blessed with a tremendous wealth, the Arabs are capable of utilizing scientific and technological know how for several purposes including self defense against their common enemy. However, their technological dependence has "enhanced their vulnerability to outside interference and reduced the degree of internal national integration."[43]

4. *Oil boom:* In the past four decades, some Arab states received huge revenues from oil production. Some of this income was used for economic development, despite the fact that in recent years some development schemes have been deferred due to the continuous tension between the Arab world and Israel,[44] and among the Arab states themselves. Moreover, in order to maintain political stability, a large percentage of oil revenues is being spent for "the substantial strengthening of the internal security apparatuses and coercive capabilities of Arab regimes."[45] Furthermore, billions of the oil dollars were, and still are, spent on purchasing the latest sophisticated weapons, mainly for the protection of these regimes from other Arab states.

5. *The United States Strategy in the Middle East:* Now that the Soviet Union has been dissolved, the U. S. strategy concentrates on: 1. military control of the Gulf Arab states which were/are willing to provide bases for American troops (e.g., for the U. S. pre-emptive war on Iraq); 2. controlling the oil prices, and even preventing possible embargo of Arab oil; and 3. maintaining Israel's military superiority. Equipped with advanced scientific and technological knowledge, Israel (according to Israeli scientists, e.g., Mordechai Vanunu and Israel Shahak) had and continues to have weapons of mass destruction, including nuclear ones. This military might is enabling Israel to continue its occupation of the West Bank and Gaza (Palestine), the Golan Heights, (Syria), and Sheb'a (Lebanon). Neither the United States nor the United Nations nor even the world public opinion are seriously pressuring Israel to withdraw from these occupied areas. Concerning the Palestinians, Chomsky states that the Palestinian "problem, their demands, their rights and prospects have not been seriously discussed in the West and are cynically disregarded."[46] Chomsky believes that "the Palestinians have suffered a severe historical injustice in that they have been deprived of a substantial part of their traditional home."[47] One has to take into account the fact that "Israel has been greatly successful in its efforts to persuade Westerners to view the Middle East and its people through Israeli eyes."[48] It seems that the Arab League is ineffective in challenging, or responding to, the Western media many of which demonstrate either unintentional ignorance of the Arabs or purposeful bias. Despite this, "increasing numbers of Americans are beginning to question the over simplified, usually inaccurate, Arab picture which they have been shown for most of their lives."[49]

6. *The absence of legitimacy:* The term state is normally associated with legitimacy, a quality that is required for any democratic state.

As a result of the reciprocal mistrust between the Arab governments and their citizens, legitimacy is practically absent and governments are noticeably "frightened." Lack of legitimacy means absence of democratic institutions.[50] Some states do not have a constitution, and, with the exception of two states, free election is unheard of. Hence the perpetuation of the unrepresentative regimes characterized by injustice, violations of human rights, and the abuse of objective media. It must be stated here that the unity which the Arabs experienced some fifty years ago "was made by representatives of governments, not by the peoples or representatives of their ideological persuasions and deeper aspirations."[51]

5.   *Arab Unity: Wardi's Hypothesis*
    In 1951, Ali al-Wardi gave a lecture to a large audience at the University of Baghdad, in which he introduced his hypothesis that the Iraqi society, and for that matter the Arab society at large, can be studied and understood through the conflict between *badawa* (nomadism) and *hadara* (urbanism).[52] Wardi acknowledges the fact that he is amending Ibn Khaldun's theory in this respect "to make his own hypothesis applicable to the present Arab society."[53]

    Wardi's hypothesis admits that some aspects of nomadism, e.g., raids, cannot be applied to our contemporary societies. His emphasis, therefore, is upon certain customs, values, and norms, e.g., *asabiyah* (unity, solidarity), pride, generosity, providing refuge, and the *use of might to make things right* which the urbanites have inherited from the nomadic Bedouins but, to a great extent, neglected them. Although *asabiyah* can be interpreted to mean coordination of activities it essentially means the overall comprehensive solidarity or unity among a highly integrated tribe or a nation characterized by cooperation, devotion, sacrifice, and democratic rules.[54] If, instead of the narrow and local *asabiyahs,* the Arab states possess the nomadic strong and comprehensive *asabiyah* they can achieve "miracles," including willingness to defend their right.[55] Like Ibn Khaldun, Wardi sees "no natural conflict between might and right: the institution of *asabiyah* successfully combines the two."[56] Wardi also follows Ibn Khaldun and Pigors in classifying rulers "into leaders and dominators."[57] When might and right are "combined in the ruler," leadership rather than domination will be achieved. Furthermore, Wardi agrees with Ibn Khaldun that "there is no place for the *asabiyah* where domination prevails." That is, "as soon as domination begins to replace leadership ... the *asabiyah* gradually loses its vigor and its binding force."[58] Wardi's observation of the Arab world confirms this conclusion: the continuous loss of binding force or unity. Hence the conflict between the genuine, strong, and comprehensive *asabiyah* and the weak, local, and narrow *asabiyah* of the Arab states which led to their disunity.

Even the nomadic love for poetry is essential. In their poems, the nomadic society praises bravery, "defiance of the strong", might, and other "achievements." On the other hand, urban Arab poets bitterly show their misfortune and the inability of their Arab states to face their enemies.[59]

Briefly stated, Wardi's hypothesis shows that in spite of the cultural clash between nomadism and urbanism in the Arab world, and despite the fact that the urbanites try to lessen their dependence on nomadic values the nomadic *asabiyah* is still useful and can be utilized to unite contemporary Arab states. That is, the more reliance on traditional comprehensive and powerful nomadic *asabiyah*, the more the likelihood that the Arabs will achieve unity based not only on democracy but also on might to defend their rights against any enemy.

NOTES

1. F. A.. Sayegh, *Arab Unity: Hope and Fulfillment* (New York: Devin-Adair, 1958), pp. 29-30. See also T. Y. Ismael, *Government and Politics of the Contemporary Middle East* (Homewood, Ill., 1970); and S. al-Khalil (Ken'an Makkiyah), *Republic of Fear* (New York: Panther Books, 1990), pp. 149-151.

2. A. Nutting, *The Arabs* (New York: Mentor Books, 1964), p. 289.

3. *Ibid.*

4. *Ibid.*, p. 292.

5. *Ibid.*, p. 293

6. F. M. Najjar, "Nationalism and Socialism," in A. Jabara and J. Terry, eds. *The Arab World: From Nationalism to Revolution* (Wilmette, Ill.: Medina University Press International, 1971), p. 7.

7. Sayegh, *op. cit.*, p. 64.

8. H. Z. Nuseibeh, *The Ideas of Arab Nationalism* (Ithaca, N. Y.: Cornell University Press, 1956), p. 207.

9. Sayegh, *op. cit.*, pp. 74-75.

10. *Ibid.*

11. *Ibid.*, pp. 74-75.

12. Nuseibeh, *op. cit.*, p. 69.

13. C. Zurayq, *Al-Wa'ayi al-Qawmi* (Beirut, 1938), p. 38. Cited in Nuseibeh, *op. cit,* pp. 69-70.

14. H. E. Tutsch, *Faces of Arab Nationalism* (Detroit: Wayne State University Press, 1965), p. 115. "A common language may not necessarily form the basis for a nation. French, Italian, Spanish, Portuguese, English, are spoken by more than one nation." *Ibid.* See also Nuseibeh, *op. cit.*, p. 70.

15. Nuseibeh, *ibid.*, p. 77. See also Sayegh, *op. cit.*, p. 74.

16. Zurayaq, *op. cit.*, p. 39. Cited in Nuseibeh, *ibid.*, p. 78.

17. R. Patai, *The Arab Mind* (New York: Hatherleigh Press, 2002), p. 221.

18. *Ibid.*

19. Zurayaq, *op. cit.* Cited in Nuseibeh, *op. cit.*, p. 93.

20. Zurayaq, *ibid.*, pp. 126-127. Cited in Nuseibeh, p. 92.

21. Sayegh, *op. cit.*, pp. 90-91. See also Tutsch, *op. cit.*, pp. 112-113.

22. Sayegh, *op. cit.*, p. 92. Emphasis added.

23. Tutsch, *op. cit.*, p. 112.

24. *Ibid.*

25. Nuseibeh, *op. cit.*, pp. 67-68, also 91; Tutsch, *op. cit.*, p. 68.

26. A. Hourani, *A History of the Arab Peoples* (New York: Warner Books, 1991), pp. 401, 405. See also Tutsch, *op. cit.*, p. 67.

27. Sayegh, *op. cit.*, p. 211.

28. *Ibid.*, p. 212.

29. *Ibid.*

30. *Ibid.*, pp. 180, 181, 187-188.

31. *Ibid.*, pp. 207-208.

32. Tutsch, *op. cit.*, p. 126, and the *New York Times,* June 16, 1962.

33. Sayegh, *op. cit.*, p. 84.

34. *Ibid.*, pp. 85-86.

35. *Ibid.*, pp. 98-99, 102-103, 104,108, 109.

36. M. C. Hudson, "Introduction," in M. C. Hudson, ed. *Middle East Dilemma* (New York: Columbia University Press, 1999), p. 13. See also Sayegh, *op. cit.*, pp. 103, 108.

37. Nutting, *op. cit.*, p. 393. Emphasis added.

38. A. K. Abdulla, "the Gulf Cooperation Council: Nature, Origin, and Process," in Hudson, *op. cit.*, p. 168. See also Hudson, *loc. cit.*; P. Noble, "The Prospects for Arab Cooperation in a Changing Regional and Global System," in Hudson, *op. cit.*, p. 76; Sayegh, *op. cit.*, p. 103; and M. A. Shuraydi, "Pan-Arabism: A Theory in Practice," in H. A. Faris, ed. *Arab Nationalism and the Future of the Arab World* (Belmont, MA.: Association of Arab-American University Graduates, 1987), p. 100.

39. Hudson, loc. cit.; G. W. Ball and D. B. Ball, *The Passionate Attachment: America's Involvement with Israel, 1947 to the Present* (New York: W. W. Norton and Co., 1992), p. 237.

40. Abdulla, *loc. cit.*

41. I. W. Zartman, "The Ups and Downs of Maghrib Unity," in Hudson *op. cit.*, pp. 182-183.

42. Terms such as "the Gulf person" (al-insan al-Khaleeji) and "the Gulf citizen" are familiar in the Persian Gulf Arab countries today. See for example, M. J. Ritha, *Sira'a al-Dawla wa al-Kabeela fi al-Khaleej al-Arabi* (Beirut: Markaz Dirasat al-Wihda al-Arabiyah, 1997), p. 95; H. Y. Nasri, *Asabiyah la Ta'ifiyah* (Beirut: Dar al-Khalam, 1982), p. 10; and K. al-Din Haseeb *et al. Mustakbal al-Umma al-Arabiyah* (Beirut: Markaz Dirasat al-Wihda al-Arabiyah,, 2002), p. 65.

43. A. B. Zahlan, "Technology: A Disintegrative Factor in the Arab World," in Hudson, *op. cit.*, p. 275. Zurayq can be considered the first Arab nationalist to emphasize this factor. See C. Zurayq, *Ma'ana al-Nekba Mujadedan* (Beirut: Dar al-Ilm lil-Malayeen, 1967), pp. 12, 14-16, 42, 124.

44. F. Baali, "The Impact of Land Reform," in Jabara and Terry, *op. cit.*, p. 31.

45. Noble, *op. cit.*, p. 82.

46. N. Chomsky, "A Radical Perspective," in Jabara and Terry, *op. cit.*, p. 187. See also E. A. Nakhleh, "Zionism and United States Foreign Policy," in Jabara and Terry, *ibid.*, p.151.

47. Chomsky, *loc. cit.* Concerning Israeli occupation of Palestinian land, former President Carter points out that "with apparent acquiescence from the Bush administration, Israeli Prime Minister ... recently announced that additional settlement units will be built and the Israeli dividing wall farther intrude into Palestinian land." (Jimmy Carter, "Quiet Negotiations Develop Possible Mideast Peace Plan," *USA Today,* November 3, 2003, p. 13A). On November 14, 2003, four former heads of Israel's security service "warned of a catastrophe for Israel if a peace deal with the Palestinians is not reached quickly, and said Prime Minister Ariel Sharon is not trying hard enough to reach a resolution to the conflict. ... They criticized the government for not setting long-term policies that could lead to a peace deal, and said Israel should strive to end its occupation of the West Bank and Gaza Strip." *Jerusalem Post,* Nov. 14, 2003. See also *Los Angels Times* of November 14, 2003.

48. M. E. Suleiman, "Perceptions of the Middle East in American News Magazines," in B. Abu-Laban and F. T. Zeadey, eds. *Arabs in America: Myths and Realities* (Wilmette, Ill.: Medina University Press International, 1975), p. 28. See also W. C. Smith, *Islam in Modern History* (New York: The New American Library, 1959), p. 103. For her research on the Arab-Israeli conflict, Janice Terry studied the attitudes of three widely circulated United States newspapers *(The New York Times, The Washington Post, and The Denver Free Press)* over a twenty-year period, 1948-1968. "The results of this study reveal a rather consistent pro-Israeli and anti Arab bias. ...Much of this was purely racist in tone, as a word-coding study would reveal statistically." J. Terry, "A Content Analysis of American Newspapers," in Jabara and Terry, *op. cit.,* pp. 94, 99, 100. After the 1973 October War, Terry conducted a somewhat similar research study of the same U. S. newspapers (in addition to two European newspapers). The major result: "in features, the pro-Israeli stance of the U. S. press becomes more pronounced." J. J. Terry, "The Western Press and the October War: A Content Analysis," in Abu-Laban and Zeadey, *op. cit.,* p. 6. For research data on prejudice and stereotyping of ethnic groups see A. al-Qazzaz, "Images of the Arab in American Social Science Textbooks," in Abu-Laban and Zeadey, *ibid.,* pp. 113-132.

49. J. A. McClure, "The Arabs: An American Awakening," in Abu-Laban and Zeadey, *ibid.,* p. 233. See also Smith, *loc. cit.*

50. F. I. Khuri, *Al-A'skar wa al-Hukum fi al-Buldan al-Arabiyah* (London: Dar al-Saqi, 1990), pp. 5, 10. See also S. al-Din Ibrahim "Azmat al-Democratiyah fi al-Watan al-Arabi," *Al-Mustakbal al-Arabi* (April 1984); G. Salamah, *Nahwa Akd Ijtima'i Arabi Jadid* (Beirut: Markaz Dirasat al-Whida al-Arabiyah, 1987), p. 9; C. Zurayaq, *Ma'ana al-Nekba Mujadedan,* pp.47-49, 104; Haseeb, *op. cit.,* pp. 235, 236, 325, 447; and Hourani, *op. cit.,* p. 406. According to Sayegh, the military officers in these countries "seriously hindered the realization of the Arab unity." Sayegh, *op. cit.,* p. 102. Democracy entails equality which the Arab woman seeks. Al-Qazzaz stresses the education of women as a necessary criterion for "the nation building process." He adds, "Without emancipating women from the bondage of illiteracy no real political, social, or economic development can take place." A. al-Qazzaz, "Education of Women in the Arab World," *Arab Perspectives* (October 1980). See also his publication, *Arab Women: Potentials and Prospects* (New York: Arab Information Center, n.d.), and Patai, *op. cit.,* pp. 354-355.

51. Sayegh, *loc. cit.*

52. A. al-Wardi, *The Iraqi Personality,* 1951; and A. al-Wardi, "Ibn Khaldun wa al-Mujtam'a al-Arabi," *A'mal Mahrajan Ibn Khaldun* (Cairo: National Center for Social Research, 1962), pp. 525, 531. Wardi believes that the Arab universities need to put more emphasis on courses dealing with the social structure, cultural change, and social problems in the Arab world that can be treated (taught) objectively. See, for example, his *Lamhat Ijtima'iyah min Tarikh al-Iraq al-Hadeeth (Social Aspects of Iraqi Modern History),* vol. 1 (Baghdad: Irshad Press, 1969), pp. 5, 318; and his *Dirasa fi Tabi'at al-Mujtam'a al-Iraqi (A Study in the Society of Iraq),* (Baghdad: al-Ani Press, 1965), pp. 5, 371, 382.

53. Wardi, "Ibn Khaldun," p. 517.

54. Wardi, *A Study in the Society of Iraq,* pp. 56-57, 70, 94, 106, and F. Baali's review of this book in the *American Sociological Review* (December 1966), p. 883; see also, *al-Manar* (Baghdad, February 14 1966), p. 6.

55. In his *Social Aspects of Iraqi Modern History,* p. 315, Wardi provides an example on the profound role of the *asabiyah* (unity): In 1920, a small, well-united, well-determined Iraqis were able to defeat and humiliate the British troops in Southern Iraq. However, this unity or *asabiyah* did not last for long.

56. F. Baali and A. Wardi, *Ibn Khaldun and Islamic Thought-Styles: A Social Perspective* (Boston: G. K. Hall, 1981), p. 51.

57. *Ibid.*

58. *Ibid.*

59. Nuseibeh, *op. cit.,* p. 15; and Patai *op. cit.,* pp. 223-24.

Chapter Four

CONCLUSION

The superficial student of knowledge tends to believe that there is no use in studying the social phenomena of the past; it is more useful to concentrate on understanding the most recent ones. Neglecting historical perspective may hinder our ability to arrive at accurate or objective generalizations concerning these phenomena. In this book, we endeavored not to belittle past ideas and phenomena, nor to neglect the historical perspective in studying them. Hence the reason for devoting the first two chapters to trace the Arab unity and disunity before, during, and after Mohammed's time. These chapters help us understand the present social, economic, and political factors affecting the movement toward unity of the Arab states. Chapter Three dealt mainly with the Arab national movement after World War One. The prime movers behind this movement were: the desire to emancipate the Arab population from foreign domination, the urge for needed socio-economic development, and the wish to fulfill a political unification. "The idea of Arab unity reflects the awakenness of Arab society, after *a long period of slumber*, fragmentation, and foreign domination; it echoes the Arab urge to catch up with the more advanced nations of the contemporary world."[1]

However, the actual attainment of unity "has been so far less far-reaching than the *idea* of Arab unity."[2] Arab unity is hindered by several factors the most important of which is the absence of legitimacy. "Effort to unify the Arab states was made by representatives of governments, not by the Arab peoples or representatives of their ideological persuasions and deeper aspirations."[3]

Something of the growing pains of Arab disunity is reflected in the tragedy of Palestine. The Palestinians are victims of betrayal and injustice committed not only by the West but by the Arab states as well. The politically powerless Arab states "failed to save Palestine from being engulfed by Israelis."[4] Today, the Palestinians play a conspicuously independent role in their destiny. In this respect, a well-known Iraqi Arab poet describes his bitter feeling toward leaders of the Arab states:

> Jerusalem is the bride of your pan-Arabism
> But why did you   allow all the criminals of the night into her room.

And stand behind the doors to stealthily hear the cries over the loss
of her virginity.
Then you withdrew your daggers and honorably boasted
And shouted at her to be silent for the protection of the family honor.
How honorable of you!
Sons of bitches
How could a raped woman be quiet?[5]

In addition to Palestinian lands, Israel also occupies the Golan Heights
(Syria) and Sheb'a (Lebanon). If implemented, the United Nations resolutions,
including Resolution 242, can solve the problem exactly the way the Israeli
representative to the U.N. in 1967 wanted: land for peace. Israel is winning the
sympathies of the media and the "Christian West;" and, as a result, forcing the
Arab to defend his character, his society, and his culture "against onslaught."[6]. It
is a truism that the Arab states did not make any serious challenge in this respect.
(They, for instance, did not clearly inform the world public that not all the
Palestinians, and for that matter not all the Arabs, are Muslims since there is a
large Christian Arab minority. They did not even provide the fact that the Arabs
are Semites, and accordingly any unjustified criticism or bias against the Arab
people constitutes anti-Semitism, even if such behavior comes from Jews!)
Intentionally or unintentionally, Israel proclaimed its ideology or contention that
"the problem of Palestine can only be solved by force."[7] Ironically, this is the
essence of Ali al-Wardi's hypothesis: What is taken by force, can only be taken
back by force, which can only be achieved through adopting the nomadic
asabiyah (unity). As we have seen (Chapters One-Three), the nomadic society
is highly integrated within tribal unit: Brotherhood, cooperation, sacrifice, and
loyalty hold among the members of the tribe, rich or poor, powerful or powerless.
The nomadic Arab is, as Hitti puts it, "a born democrat."[8] Proud of his tribe as a
strong social unit, the nomad cannot understand right without might behind it.
Briefly stated, Wardi asserts that these cultural elements or behavior patterns are
what the Arab states need in working together toward unity. To a great extent,
Wardi's hypothesis is correct. When the Arabs wanted to liberate their occupied
lands they adopted the nomadic *asabiyah,* made "careful planning and serious
determination,"[9] and waged the October 1973 war. That event by itself shattered
the myth that Arabs cannot unite, and proved Ibn Khaldun's and Wardi's
hypotheses that right can be achieved through might. That same event
encouraged the Arabs to impose their will against the West through the short-
lived embargo on the export of their oil.

As we have seen in the previous chapter, exceptions are not the rules.
Today, Arab rulers do not discuss Arab unity despite the fact that the Arab states
had and still have many opportunities to unite. These states are "governed by
divisiveness, rivalries, ideological squabbling, bickering, and a deep sense of

mistrust and deception."[10] This is in addition to "the selfishness inherent in the imperfection"[11]of these states, almost all of which perpetuate an autocratic rule. They spend their richness to buy the latest weapons, not for the purpose of fighting their common enemy, but to enhance their control and to repress democratic movements. "Ruling groups had been successful in creating and maintaining their own *asabiyah* or solidarity directed towards acquiring and keeping power."[12] The irony is that "even the most stable and the longest-lasting regimes ... might prove to be fragile."[13] An Arab poet painted a gloomy picture of this familiar Arab situation:[14]

> Arise, O Arabs, from sleep awake!
> Knee-deep we're sunk in misery's lake

The Arab world area is approximately 5.25 million square miles[14] divided into 22 states, including Palestine. No two Arab states are united or federated. "Even Pan-Arab nationalists are of divided opinion on the best way to accomplish unity; whether to form a confederation of sovereign states, a federation or federal union in which each state would renounce its sovereignty but keep its separate identity, or to join closely in a single centralized state."[16]

The fragmentation of the Arab world into several political units is an abnoramality.[17] A single nation can be achieved if the local, narrow, *asabiyahs* of the Arab states are combined in one large, powerful, and unified *asabiyah*,[18] based not only on mere "cooperation" and coordination of activities but also on everyone's devotion and sacrifice. That is, the loyalty is to the single Arab nation. Legitimacy is a priority prerequisite, and accordingly democracy is expected to be respected and upheld. Citizens are guaranteed the needed freedom of expression, justice, and equality. The new single nation can use the oil revenues to improve the socio-economic conditions of its citizens, strengthen its capabilities and capacities for self-defense against any enemy, and instill the needed pride and dignity.

Some writers believe that Arab unity cannot be indefinitely arrested.[19] In our opinion, this single Arab nation may be "a faraway dream."[20] On the basis of our observation and knowledge of the Arab unity and disunity in the past and present (Chapters One-Three) we conclude that a unity may come, but it is doubtful that it would last for a long time. What the Arabs need today and for a long time is another Mohammed. Otherwise, they may have to keep waiting for the *Mahdi*, the "expected" future savior.

NOTES

1. F. A. Sayegh, *Arab Unity*: Hope and Fulfillment (New York: Devin-Adair, 1948), p. 214. Emphasis added

2. *Ibid.*, p. 216. Emphasis added

3. *Ibid.*, p.102.

4. A. Nutting, *The Arabs* (New York: Mentor Book, 1964), p. 393.

5. M. al-Nawab, *watariyat Laylyia* (1975), pp. 76-77. The English translation in M. A. Shuraydi, "Pan-Arabism: A Theory in Practice," in H. A. Faris, ed. *Arab Nationalism and the future of the Arab World* (Belmont, MA: Association of Arab-American University Graduates, 1987), p. 103. Some 55 years ago, the present writer published an article titled "Tasreehat" ("Official Statements") in the widely-read Iraqi magazine *Al-Wadi*. The article criticizes the Arab leaders, especially those of the Arab League, for their ineffective activity and unproductive slogans and statements concerning Palestine and Arab unity. In this respect, leaders of the Arab states show consistency!

6. W. C. Smith, *Islam in Modern History* (New York: The New American Library, 1959), pp. 111, 117. See Chapter Three, ft. 48.

7. H. E. Tutsch, *Faces of Arab Nationalism* (Detroit: Wayne State University Press, 1965), p. 63. According to the Jewish scholar and Rabbi Elmer Berger, the following was printed as (Pamphlet #1, Friends of Jerusalem, New York, 1968): "Israel, tends to spread utter confusion within the Jewish community and in the outside world because its policies and actions are carried out under the name of Israel, which is the historical designation of the Jewish people, even when those policies and actions are diametrically opposed to Jewish tradition, Jewish religious (Torah) laws and the real interests of the Jewish people. Indeed, the very establishment of this secular national "Jewish" state constitutes a break with Jewish tradition and with the norms laid down for the Jewish People in talmudic and rabbinic laws." See E. Berger, "Theological and Religious Implications of Zionism in Palestine," in A. Jabara and J. Terry, eds. The Arab World from Nationalism to Revolution (Wilmette, Ill.: Medina University Press Inernational 1971), p. 141.

8. P. K. Hitti, *The Arabs*: A Short History (Chicago: Henry Regnery, 1949), p. 19.

9. A. Hourani, *A History of the Arab Peoples* (New York: Warner Books 1991), p. 418.

10. Shuraydi, *op. cit.*, p. 100.

11. Sayegh, *op. cit.*, p. 83.

12. Hourani, *op. cit.*, p. 449. Emphasis added.

13. *Ibid.*, pp. 455 - 456.

14. This poem by Ibrahim al-Yaziji was written in 1868. See Tutsch, *op. cit.*, p. 121.

15. H. S. Haddad and B. K. Nijim, eds. *The Arab World:* A Handbook (Wilmette, Ill.: Medina Press, 1978), p. 1. See also N. Alwash, *Al-Watan al-Arabi* (Beirut: Markaz Dirasat al-Wihda al-Arabiyah, 1986).

16. Tutsch, *op. cit.*, p. 87.

17. See Sayegh, *op. cit.*, p. 76.

18. *Asabiyah* and nationalism may be considered analogous. Both emphasize identity, loyalty, a sense of belonging, and aspiration. F. Baali, "Asabiyah," *The Oxford Encyclopedia of the Modern Islamic World* (New Yoork and Oxford: Oxford University Press, 1995), p. 140.

19. See Sayegh, *op. cit.*, 212; and E. W. Said, "Palestine and the Future of the Arabs," in Faris, *op. cit.*, p. 34.

20. H. S. Haddad and B. K. Nijim, "An Historical Survey," in Haddad and Nijim, *op. cit.*, p. 32.

BIBLIOGRAPHY

Abd al-Raziq, A. *Al-Islam wa Usul al-Hukum*. Cairo: Misr Press, 1925.

Abdulla, Abdul Kahleq. "The Gulf Cooperation Council," in M.C. Hudson, ed. *Middle East Dilemma*. New York: Columbia University Press, 1999.

Abu-Yusuf, Y. *Kitab al-Kharaj*. Cairo: Salafiyah Press, A. H. 1347.

Alayili, A. *Tarikh al-Husayn*. Beirut. Irfan Bookstore, n. d.

Ali, Ameer. *The Spirit of Islam*. London: Christophers, 1949.

Ali bin Abi-Talib. *Nahj al-Balaghah*, ed. M. Abduh. Cairo: Istiqamah Press, n. d.

Amin, Ahmed. *Fajr al-Islam*. Cairo: Lajnat al-Ta-lif, 1945.

_____. *Duha al-Islam*. Cairo: Lajnat al-Ta'lif, 1938.

_____. *Thuhr al-Islam*, vol. 1. Cairo: Lajnat al-Ta'lif, 1945.

Aqqad, Abbas al-. *Abqariyat al-Imam*. Cairo: Ma'arif Press, 1952.

Arnold, T. W. *The Preaching of Islam*. Lahore: Shirkat-i-Qualam, 1956.

Baali, Fuad. "The Impact of Land Reform," in A. Jabara and J. Terry, eds. *The Arab World from Nationalism to Revolution*. Wilmette, Ill.: Medina University Press International, 1971.

_____. Review of A. Wardi's *Dirasah fi Tabi'at al-Mujtama' al-Iraqi, American Sociological Review*, vol. 31 (December 1966).

_____. "*Asabiya,*" *The Oxford Encyclopedia of the Modern Islamic World*. New York and Oxford: Oxford University Press, 1995.

_____, and Ali Wardi. *Ibn Khaldun and Islamic Thought-Styles: A Social Perspective*. Boston: G. K. Hall, 1981.

Ball, George W. and Douglas B. Ball. *The Passionate Attachment: America's Involvement with Israel*. New York: W. W. Norton and Co., 1992.

Berger, Elmer. "Theological and Religious Implications of Zionism in Palestine," in A. Jabara and J. Terry, eds. *The Arab World from Nationalism to Revolution*. Wilmette, Ill.: Medina University Press International, 1971.

Browne, Edward G. *A Literary History of Persia*. New York: Charles Scribner's Sons, 1902.

Chomsky, Noam. "A Radical Perspective," in A. Jabara and J. Terry, eds. *The Arab World from Nationalism to Revolution*. Wilmette, Ill.: Medina University Press International, 1971.

Donaldson, D. M. *Aqidat al-Shi'a*. Cairo: Sa'ada Press, 1933.

Durant, W. *The Story of Civilization*. New York: Simon and Schuster, 1942.

Durkheim, Emile. *The Division of Labor in Society,* trans. by George Simpson. New York: The Free Press, 1933.

Enan, Mohammad Abdullah. *Ibn Khaldun: His Life and Work*. Lahore: Sh. Muhammad Ashraf, 1969.

Goeje, M. de. "Arabia," *Encyclopedia of Islam*. Leiden: Brill, 1913.

Grunebaum, G. E. von. *Medieval Islam*. Chicago: University of Chicago Press, 1946.

Haddad, Hassan S. and Basheer K. Nijim, eds. *The Arab World: A Handbook*. Wilmette, Ill.: Medina Press, 1978.

Haseeb, K. al-Din et al. *Mustakbul al-Umma al-Arabiyah*. Beirut: Markaz Dirasat al-Wihda al-Arabiyah, 2002.

Heberle, Rudolf. "The Sociology of Georg Simmel: The Forms of Social Interaction," in H. E. Barnes, ed. *An Introduction to the History of Sociology*. Chicago: University of Chicago Press, 1948.

Hitti, Philip K. *History of the Arabs*. London: Macmillan, 1946.

_____. The Arabs: *A Short History*. Chicago: Henry Regnery, 1956.

_____. *Makers of Arab History*. New York: Harper, 1968.

Hourani, Albert. *A History of the Arab Peoples*. New York: Warner Books, 1991.

Hudson, Michael C. "Introduction," in M. D. Hudson, ed. *Middle East Dilemma*. New York: Columbia University Press, 1999.

Husari, Sati' al-. *Dirasat an Muqaddimat Ibn Khaldun*. Beirut: Kashshaf Press, 1943.

Hussein, Taha. *Etude analytique et critique de la philosophie sociale d'Ibn Khaldoun*. *Paris*: A. Pedone, 1917.

Ibn Khaldun, Abd al-Rahman. *Al-Muqaddimah*. Beirut: Dar al-Kashshaf, n. d.

_____. *The Muqaddimah: An Introduction to History*, trans. by Franz Rosenthal Princeton: Princeton University Press, 1967.

_____. *Kitab al-Ibar*. Cairo: Bulaq Press, A. H. 1384.

Ibrahim, Sa'ad al-Din. "Azmat al-Democratiyah fi al-Watan al-Arabi," *Al-Mustakbal al-Arabi* (April 1984).

Ismael, T. Y. *Government and Politics of the Contemporary Middle East*. Homewood, Ill., 1970.

Issawi, Charles. *An Arab Philosophy of History: Selections from the Prolegomena of Ibn Khaldun of Tunis*, 1332-1406. London: John Murray, 1950.

Khadduri, Majid. *The Law of War and Peace in Islam*. London: Luzac, 1940.

Khalil Samir al-. (Ken'an Makkiyah). *Republic of Fear*. New York: Panther Books, 1990.

Khuri, Fuad I. *Al-A'skar wa al-Hukum fi al-Buldan al-Arabiyah*. London: Dar al-Saqi, 1990.

Kohn, H. "Messianism," *Encyclopedia of Social Sciences*, vol. 10, 1931.

Koran, The.

Lacoste, Yves. *Ibn Khaldoun: Naissance de l'histoire passé du tiers monde*. Arabic trans. by M. Sulaiman. Beirut: Ibn Khaldun House. 1973.

Lahbabi, Muhammed Aziz. "Isalat al-Manhajiyah ind Ibn Khaldun," *Mahrajan Ibn Khaldun*. Casablanca: Dar el-Kitab. 1962.

Lane-Poole, S. *The Speeches and Table-Talk of the Prophet Mohammed*. London: Macmillan, 1905.

Levy, Reuben. *An Introduction to the Sociology of Islam*, vol. 1. London: Williams and Norgate, 1931.

Macdonald, D. G. *The Development of Muslim Theology, Jurisprudence, and Constitutional Theory*. New York: Charles Scribner's Sons, 1903.

_____. "Ilm," *Encyclopedia of Islam*. Leiden: Brill, 1927.

_____. "Isa," *Encyclopedia of Islam*, vol. 2. Leiden: Brill, 1927.

Maghribi, A. Q. al-. *Al-Akhlaq wa al-Wajibat*. Cairo; Salafiyah Press, A. H. 1347.

Margoliouth, D. S. "Mahdi," *Encyclopedia of Religion and Ethics*, vol. 8, 1908.

Masse, H. *Islam*. New York: Putnam, 1938.

McClure, James A. "The Arabs: An American Awakening," in B. Abu-Laban and F. T. Zeadey, eds. *Arabs in America: Myths and Realities*. Wilmette, Ill.: Medina University Press International, 1975.

Mead, George H. *Mind, Self and Society*. Chicago: University of Chicago Press, 1934.

Miqdadi, Darwish al-. *Tarikh al-Ummat al-Arabiyah*. Baghdad: Ma'arif Press, 1932.

Muir, W. *Annals of the Early Caliphate*. London: Smith, Elder and Co., 1883.

Nackleh, Emile E. "Zionism and United States Foreign Policy," in A. Jabara and J. Terry, eds. *The Arab World from Nationalism to Revolution*. Wilmette, Ill.: Medina University Press International,1971.

Najjar, Fauzi M. "Nationalism and Socialism," in A. Jabara and J. Terry, eds. *The Arab World from Nationalism to Revolution*. Wilmette, Ill.: Medina University Press International, 1971.

Nasri, Hani Yahya. *Asabiyah la Ta'ifiyah*. Beirut: Dar al-Khalam, 1982.

Nawab, Muthaffar al-. *Watariyat Laylyia*, 1975.

Nicholson, R. A. *Literary History of the Arabs*. Cambridge: University Press, 1930.

Noble, Paul. "The Prospect for Arab Cooperation in a Changing Regional and Global System," in M. C. Hudson, ed. *Middle East Dilemma*. New York: Columbia University Press, 1999.

Nour, M. A. M. "Ibn Khaldun Ka-mufakir Ijtima'i Arabi," *A'mal mahrajan Ibn Khaldun*. Cairo: National Center for Social Research, 1962.

Nuseibeh, Hazem Zaki. *The Ideas of Arab Nationalism*. Ithaca, N. Y.: Cornell University Press, 1956.

Nutting, Anthony. *The Arabs*. New York: Mentor Books, 1964.

O'Leary, De Lacy. *Arabia Before Muhammad*. New York: Dutton, 1927.

Patai, Raphael. *The Arab Mind*. New York: Hatherleigh Press, 2002.

Pigors, Paul. *Leadership and Domination*. New York: Houghton Mifflin, 1935.

Qazzaz, Ayad al-. "Images of the Arab in American Social Science Textbook," in B. Abu-Laban and F. T. Zeadey, eds. *Arabs in America: Myths and Realities*. Wilmette, Ill.: Medina University Press International, 1975.

————. "Education of Women in the Arab world," *Arab Perspectives* (October 1980).

Rabi', Muhammad Mahmoud. *The Political Theory of Ibn Khaldun*. Leiden: E. J. Brill, 1967.

Ritha, M. Jawad. *Sir'a al-Dawla wa al-kabeela fi al-Khaleej al-Arabi*. Beirut: Markaz Dirasat al-Wihda al-Arabiyah, 1997.

Ritter, Hellmut. "Irrational Solidarity Groups: A Socio-psychological Study in Connection with Ibn Khaldun," *Oriens*, vol. 1. (1948).

Rosenthal, Franz. "Introduction" to Ibn Khaldun, *The Muqaddimah: An Introduction to History*, tans. by Franz Rosenthal. Princeton: Princeton University Press, 1967.

Sahhar, A. J. al-. *Ahl al-Bayt*. Cairo: Misr Press, 1968.

Said, Edward W. "Palestine and the Future of the Arabs," in H. A. Faris, ed. *Arab Nationalism and the Future of the Arab World*. Belmont, MA: Association of Arab-American University Graduates, 1987.

Salamah, Ghasan. *Nahwa Akd Ijtima'i Arabi Jadid*. Beirut: Markaz Dirasat al-Whida al-Arabiyah, 1987.

Santillana, D. de. "Laws and Society," in T. Arnold and A. Guillaume, ed. *Legacy of Islam*. London: Oxford University Press, 1931.

Sayegh, Fayez A. *Arab Unity: Hopes and Fulfillment*. New York: Devin-Adair Co., 1958.

Schacht, J. "Mohammed," *Encyclopedia of Social Sciences*, vol. 10, 1931.

_____. "Sharia," *Encyclopedia of Islam*, 1934.

_____. "Usul," *Encyclopedia of Islam*. Leiden: Brill, 1934.

Sharaf al-Din, A. H. *Al-Fusul al-Muhimmah*. Saida: Irfan Press, A. H. 1347.

Sherwani, Haron Khan. *Studies in Muslim Political Thought and Administration*. Lahore: Sh. Muhammed Ashraf, 1963.

Shuraydi, Muhammad A. "Pan-Arabism: A Theory in Practice," in Hani A. Faris, ed. *Arab Nationalism and the Future of the Arab World*. Belmont, MA: Association of Arab-American University Graduates, 1987.

Simon, Heinrich, *Ibn Khalduns Wissenschaft von der Menschlichen Kultur*. Leipzig, 1959.

Smith, Wilfred Cantwell. *Islam in Modern History*. New York: The New American Library, 1959.

Smith, W. Robertson. *Kinship and Marriage in Early Arabia*. London: Adams and Charles Black, 1903.

Sorokin, P. A. et al. *A Systematic Source Book in Rural Sociology*, vol. 1. Minneapolis: University of Minnesota Press, 1930.

Speyer, H. "Yahud," *Encyclopedia of Islam*, vol. 4. 1934.

Strothmann, R. "Shia," *Encyclopedia of Islam*. Leiden: Brill, 1934.

Subayti, A. al-. *Abu Dhar*. Tahran: Sa'adi Press, 1945.

Suleiman, Michael W. "Perceptions of the Middle East in American News Magazines," in B. Abu-Laban and F. T. Zeadey, eds. *Arabs in America: Myths and Realities*. Wilmette, Ill." Medina University Press International, 1975.

Terry, Janice, J. "The Western Press and the October War: A Content Analysis," in B. Abu-Laban and F. T. Zeadey, eds. *Arabs in America: Myths and Realities*. Wilmette, Ill.: Medina University Press International, 1975.

_____. "A Content Analysis of American Newspapers," in A. Jabara and J. Terry, eds. *The Arab World from Nationalism to Revolution*. Wilmette, Ill.: The Medina University Press International, 1971.

Toynbee, Arnold J. *A Study of History*, vol. 3. New York: Oxford University Press, 1962.

Tutsch, Hans E. *Faces of Arab Nationalism*. Detroit: Wayne State University Press, 1965.

Vaux, B. Carra de. "Dajjal," *Encyclopedia of Islam*, vol. 1. Leiden: Brill, 1913.

Wardi, Ali al-. *The Iraqi Personality*. 1951.

_____. "Ibn Khaldun wa al-Mujtam'a al-Arabi" *A'mal Mahrajan Ibn Khaldun*. Cairo: National Center for Social Research, 1962.

_____. *Dirasa fi Tabi'at al-Mujtam'a al-Iraqi* (A Study in the Society of Iraq). Baghdad: Ani Press, 1965.

_____. *Lamhat Ijtima'iyah min Tarikh al-Iraq al-Hadeeth* (Social Aspects of Iraqi Modern History), vol. 1. Baghdad: al-Irshad Press, 1969.

Wells, H. G. *The Outline of History*. New York: Garden City Publishing Co., 1932.

Wensinck, A. J. "Masih," *Encyclopedia of Islam*, vol. 3. Leiden: Brill, 1936.

Wiese, L. von. *Systematic Sociology*. New York: Arno Press, 1974.

Will, Edouard. Review of G. Nebel's *Sokrates, Revue Historique* (October-December 1970).

Zahlan, Antoine B. "Technology: A Disintegrative Factor in the Arab World," in M. C. Hudson, ed. *Middle East Dilemma*. New York: Columbia University Press, 1999.

Zartman, I. William. "The Ups and Downs of Maghrib Unity," in M. C. Hudson, ed. *Middle East Dilemma*. New York: Columbia University Press, 1999.

Zaydan, Jurji. *Tarikh al-Tamaddum al-Islami*. Cairo: Hilal Press, 1902.

Zayn, Muhammad Husayn. *Al-Shi'ah fi al-Tarikh*. Saida: Irafan Press, 1938.

Zurayq, C. *Ma'ana al-Nekba Mujadedan*. Beirut: al-Ilm lil-Malayeen, 1967.

_____. *Al-Wa'ayi al-Qawmi*. Beirut, 1938.

ABOUT THE AUTHOR

The author, naturalized American, was born in Baghdad, Iraq. He received his M.A. and Ph.D. degrees in the United States and began his teaching career at Middle Tennessee State University. He also taught at the University of Baghdad, University of Florida, American University of Beirut, and Kuwait University. Currently he is Professor Emeritus, Western Kentucky University. The author has published several books, some of which were printed by the University of Florida Press, Rand McNally, Appleton-Century-Crofts, Prentice-Hall, G.K. Hall, the State University of New York Press, and University Press of America.

INDEX